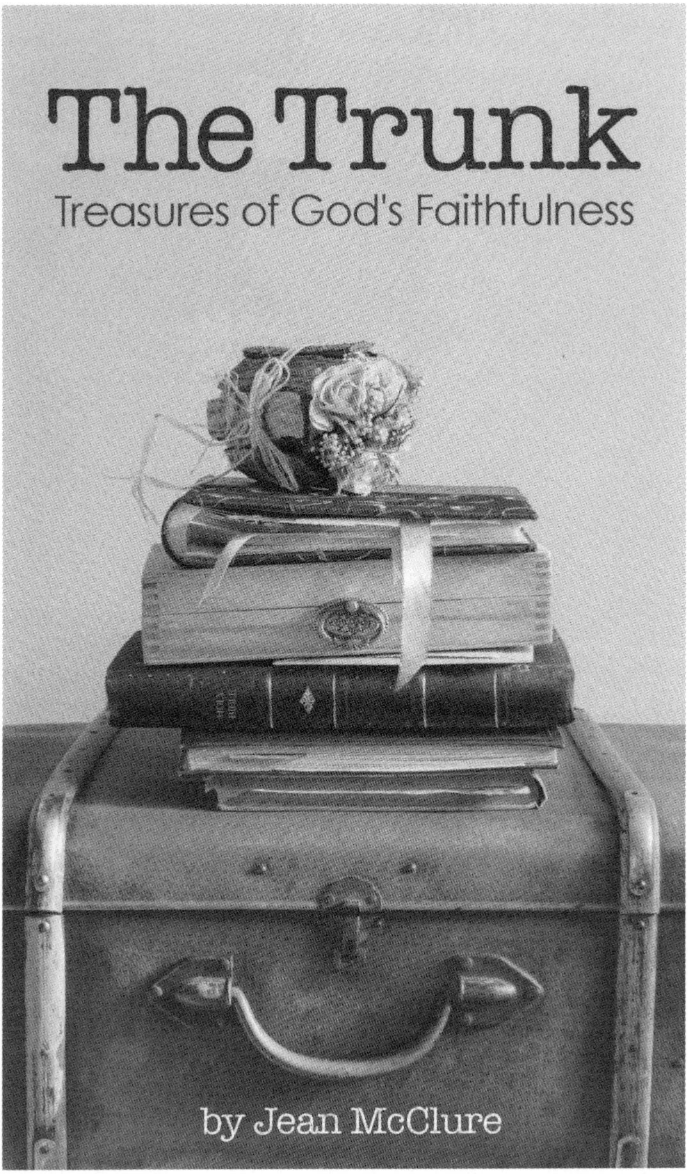

The Trunk
Treasures of God's Faithfulness

by Jean McClure

THE TRUNK
Treasures of God's Faithfulness
by Jean McClure

©2015 Jean McClure. All rights reserved.
No part of this book may be reproduced in any written, electronic, recording, or photocopying form without the prior permission of the author.

Calvary Way Ministries
P.O. Box 12282
Newport Beach, CA 92660
www.calvaryway.com

All Scripture quotations, unless otherwise noted, are taken from the New King James Version. Copyright © 1982 by Thomas Nelson, Inc. Used by permission. All rights reserved.

Scripture quotations marked KJV are taken from the King James Version of the Bible.

Scripture quotations marked NIV are taken from *The Holy Bible, New International Version*. Copyright© 1973, 1978, 1984. International Bible Society. Used by permission of Zondervan Publishing House. All rights reserved.

Editing and internal layout: Angie Emma
Cover design: Joanna Liegel
Cover photo and internal artwork: © Thinkstock

ISBN: 978-0-9835950-4-5

Printed in the United States of America

*I rejoice at Your word
as one who finds great treasure.*
Psalm 119:162

Contents

	Foreword	1
	Introduction	3
1.	My Family Roots	9
2.	Mount Hermon: Rats, Ants, and Salvation	19
3.	Praying with Childlike Faith	25
4.	Boarding School	29
5.	Learning for Life	37
6.	Capernwray, England	45
7.	Provision to the Penny	51
8.	Children—Firstborn	55
9.	The Jesus People Movement	61
10.	Michael's Miracles and the Crippled Children's Society	69
11.	Our Mountaintop Season in Lake Arrowhead	77
12.	Redlands, California	91
13.	Serpents and Poison	97
14.	The Adventures of Donny	103
15.	San Jose, California	117
16.	God's Message Hasn't Changed	125
17.	"Never Get Better"	133
18.	Miracles in the Silicon Valley	137
19.	A Refuge in All Our Ways	145
20.	He Knows Our Dwelling Place: Blain Court	153
21.	The Pilgrim Years	157
22.	Final Reflections	175

Foreword

*Many, O LORD my God, are Your wonderful works
which You have done; and Your thoughts toward us
cannot be recounted to You in order; if I would declare
and speak of them, they are more than can be numbered.
I have not hidden Your righteousness within my heart;
I have declared Your faithfulness and Your salvation;
I have not concealed Your lovingkindness
and Your truth from the great assembly.*
Psalm 40:5, 10

My husband, Joe, and I have known Don and Jean McClure for over thirty years. They have been our best friends and a constant source of godly wisdom and encouragement to us. The Lord knew that as a young pastor's wife, I would need another pastor's wife to learn from and in whom I could confide. Jean has been that friend and confidant for me all of these years. We have prayed together, laughed together, cried together, and trusted in God's Word together through so many seasons in our lives.

THE TRUNK

Jean has opened God's Word and shared with me many amazing stories of how He has worked in her life. Just by listening to all He has done for her, my faith has been strengthened, and my love for God's Word has grown deeper.

I am delighted that God has put it on her heart to write these stories down so you will be blessed and encouraged by them as well.

> *Thy testimonies have I taken as an heritage for ever: for they are the rejoicing of my heart. I have inclined mine heart to perform thy statutes alway, even unto the end.*
> Psalm 119:111-112 (KJV)

Jean loves God's Word, and it is reflected in all she does in her life. Here in these pages, her life story is briefly opened to you—there is so much more she could have shared! She has reached into the trunk of her life and taken out many lessons that God has taught her. Some of these lessons are taken from everyday circumstances and others from extremely hard times in her life. They are priceless treasures, written in a very practical way, from her heart and God's to yours! I am confident you will be blessed as you read this book. It might very well become one of your favorite books, one you will refer to all the time! I know I will!

Thank you, friend, for sharing your heart and life with all of us!

Cathy Focht
Calvary Chapel of Philadelphia

Introduction

I will sing of the mercies of the L<small>ORD</small> forever:
with my mouth will I make known
thy faithfulness to all generations.
Psalm 89:1 (KJV)

The book you hold in your hands was inspired by a thought and a prayer of my mother-in-law, Carol. I lovingly dedicate this book to her. As I write this, she is ninety-one years old, and is living in an Alzheimer's home with constant care because she suffers from dementia. I suppose some mother-in-laws can be challenging and hard to get along with, but mine is an exceptional and rather wonderful woman! I dearly love my mother-in-law. She is a godly woman and a prayer warrior. Carol knows her Lord and knows His Word inside and out, and has helped so many. God has given her a very special gift through prayer of hearing His voice and sharing His truth and wisdom. She led the intercessory prayer meeting for Kay Smith at Calvary Chapel of Costa Mesa for close to thirty years. When anyone ever shared a problem with her, she would immediately stop and pray. What an example! She has always done this for me, and I will always be grateful. And even there in the retirement home, suffering from dementia, the Lord continues to use her. Our minds may go, but the Spirit of the Lord always has our souls.

This truth became very real to her one day as she cried out to the Lord in fear and desperation as her memory began to slip. She was noticing that she was forgetting things, and not being as aware of things around her as she normally was. She asked the Lord if she was losing her mind. The Lord gave her a vision of a healthy, green and beautiful plant. It was a strong vine with many leaves covering it and a large bunch of leaves at the top.

As she watched, the Lord took His hand and ran it up the vine. As He did this the leaves all along the vine turned brown and fell off. He stopped His hand just short of the top and didn't touch those leaves. All that was left was the large bunch of leaves at the top. He told her, *Yes, Carol, you are losing your mind. You will forget many things: your memories, your friends, and your family, and those things that made up your days. These are the leaves that are dying and falling off. But that is Me at the top. I will remain, and I will never leave you or forsake you. My green leaves will be there forever.* And just as He promised, God has kept this word to her in this challenging season of her life. His promise is that He will never leave us or forsake us. Still today she is radiating the Lord. Recently, as I was reading Scripture to her, she leaned all the way

INTRODUCTION

forward; she couldn't get close enough to me in her desire to hear God's Word.

> *For he shall be like a tree planted by the waters,*
> *which spreads out its roots by the river,*
> *and will not fear when heat comes; but its leaf will be*
> *green, and will not be anxious in the year of drought,*
> *nor will cease from yielding fruit.*
> Jeremiah 17:8

Not long ago, my husband, Don, and I picked up his mom and dad to take them to his dad's ninety-fourth birthday party. I rode with Carol in the backseat so we could visit along the way. She loves to visit.

As we drove she asked me, "What's going on with you these days? How are all your children?"

"The kids are doing well, Mom," I said. "But I am speaking at a retreat this weekend in Santa Barbara and would love your prayers. I am trying to put a message together for the ladies."

Immediately, she began praying out loud; this was not unusual for her. She had done this all the years I had known her. She prayed a prayer I desperately needed to hear, and I have never forgotten what she said. Everything I needed she prayed for with wisdom and faith. It amazed me to listen to the clarity and truth that came from her lips despite her increasing dementia. We are slowly losing her, and I so desperately miss her! But even as her mental state is disappearing, God spoke clearly through her and gave peace to my heart.

THE TRUNK

"Lord," she prayed, "as Jean is speaking this weekend to those women, let her take out of the trunk of her life those things that You put in her all these years; those things You have shown her. May she freely share them. May they bless others."

As she prayed, I pictured myself in an attic opening an old steamer trunk where I had stored my treasures over the years. I carefully pulled things out and examined them one at a time. Each item I held in my hands told a different story. They each reminded me of something amazing that God had done. They were like stones of remembrance to God's faithfulness over the years (see Joshua 4). Her prayer for me that day was the inspiration behind this book.

I want to invite you to open this trunk of treasures with me as I recount the myriad ways God has led me, taught me, corrected me, inspired me, protected me, and been faithful to me. My life has been an incredible journey as I have walked with the Lord and served Him all these years. He has shown me mercy and love and been faithful in each and every detail of my story. It is in the dark valleys that I see Him most clearly. His Word sheds piercing light when the journey has been difficult and I can't seem to find any answers myself. Like David I can say: "Your Word is a lamp to my feet and a light to my path" (Psalm 119:105).

God's Word is full of treasures for us to discover and hold on to. He told His children to write about their history—the miracles, the battles, the victories, and the defeats. Those lessons and stories have spoken to my heart thousands of years later!

INTRODUCTION

They have encouraged me in my faith. They have exhorted and blessed me. Testimonies in the lives of others are written in God's Word from Genesis through Revelation.

It is my hope and prayer that as you read the stories of my life, taken out of the trunk of my journey, that you will be encouraged to trust God more, to know Him more personally, and to dig into His Word for yourself.

Remember the word to Your servant, upon which
You have caused me to hope. This is my comfort in my
affliction, for Your word has given me life. Your statutes
have been my song in the house of my pilgrimage.
Psalm 119:49-50, 54

1

My Family Roots

*I have been young, and now am old; yet I have not seen
the righteous forsaken, nor his descendants begging bread.*
Psalm 37:25

My parents grew up during a time when the world was changing and advancing dramatically; it was the age of men going to the moon and telescopes seeing into other galaxies. The 20th century was an incredible time. There were so many advances, inventions, and discoveries; from the first automobile to airplanes, to man reaching the moon, to heart transplants. Much of this shaped who they were and how they thought. My father's first job was driving a horse and buggy in St. Paul, Minnesota, to pick up fresh produce and deliver it to the local market. He went on from there to become a medical doctor and earn five degrees, including becoming a Fellow (which was a great honor in the medical field at that time). He became a surgeon and invented Tucks (which many people have thanked him for!).

My parents' story really begins overseas. Looking back, I can see that God's hand was on their lives from the very beginning. Both of my grandmothers (and one grandfather) came from Europe into New York at the age of sixteen. One came from Norway; the other came from Heidelberg, Germany. It was rumored that my Norwegian grandmother, Dora, came because her parents did not like her boyfriend; so they sent her to America with her brother to start a new life in this new country.

My father was born when his mother was in her forties and her husband was fifty-three. My German grandmother had my mom—the last of twelve children—when she was also was in her forties. Interestingly, I was also the youngest, and my parents were in their forties when I was born.

I never knew either of my grandfathers. They had passed away long before I was ever a thought. My dad's dad was born in 1859 just before the Civil War. My grandparents had all settled in St. Paul and Minneapolis, and my parents were born in the very early 1900s.

In that era, before television and Billy Graham Crusades, there were tent meetings where preachers and evangelists would come and speak for a series of meetings.

At the age of seventeen, my aunt Frieda (my mom's sister) went to one of these meetings in Minneapolis and met Christ.

She was so excited that she went home and invited my mom to go the next night. "No!" she said, "I don't think so." She was only twelve and wasn't interested. "I'll give you a watch if you will go with me," Frieda pleaded. That did it! My mother and grandmother went and both came to saving faith in Christ that night, thanks to Aunt Frieda.

Frieda bought the watch as promised and spent the next three months paying it off. That was the beginning of Christian roots in my family. You never know where it will start in a family. Perhaps it will be with you! How lovely when it continues from there to the following generations.

A few years later, my mom was in nurse's training at the university when she discovered her precious watch had been stolen from her dorm room. She was heart-sick and so distracted by it that she showed up late to her next class. In those days, if you were late to class you were locked out. So she and her roommate sat outside on the steps waiting until class was over.

Interestingly, God even used this seemingly little situation in His sovereign plan. That was the special day when my parents first met. My dad, who was also in medical school at the university studying to become a doctor, was working on a cadaver in a nearby lab. When he came outside, he saw my mom. They met and soon after fell in love. They decided to wait until Dad finished medical school and my mom finished her nurse's training to get married. Mom had been going to church, but no one had told her she shouldn't marry a non-Christian. So it was after they were married that she would trudge through snow to a Christian neighbor's house to pray for Dad's salvation.

On his first day of medical school, his professor said, "No one here believes in God, do they?" As my dad told me the story he said, "We all looked up to our professors and wanted to believe everything they told us." And he mentioned later that he often wondered what that professor would face on Judgment Day for all of those years of leading students astray and planting doubt in their minds. Those "professing themselves to be wise, they became fools" (Romans 1:22). They will be accountable for what they taught and how they influenced the next generation.

One day, Dad got very sick. He had pneumonia with a 105 F fever. He realized he could die. Every day the minister came to see him (sent by my mom). It was hard for him to believe in something that required blind faith because he was so educated in the sciences. To him, everything must be proven in a test tube and under microscopes.

He knew the mind and the human body were far too perfect, too intricate. He knew there must be Something, Someone. He went to church but couldn't understand it.

As he laid there in the hospital bed, perhaps he remembered the time when he went to church with Mom. As the service began, the speaker announced the title of the sermon: "Oh Philip, how long have you been with me and have not known Me?" (taken from John 14:9).

My dad's name was Philip Anderson. He almost fell off the pew and accused my mom of telling the preacher about him. She hadn't. But God was calling his heart. Often when he was shaving, he quoted the Scripture, "Though your sins are as scarlet, they shall be as white as snow" (Isaiah 1:18). He could not figure out what that meant!

So there he was, in his early thirties, in the hospital with a 105 F fever. My mom was crying as she sat beside him. He asked her, "Are you crying because I am dying?" She said, "No. I am not crying because you are dying, but because of where you are going to go if you die." Her response really shocked my dad. The preacher came one more time to visit him, and was pretty tired of coming and not getting anywhere. So he bluntly said, "Phil, don't you want to be saved?" Dad knew at that moment it was his last chance. If he said no again he would not get another opportunity.

He, that being often reproved hardeneth his neck, shall suddenly be destroyed, and that without remedy.
Proverbs 29:1 (KJV)

So he said, "Jesus, if You are there and You are real, I ask You to forgive my sins and come into my life and be my Savior. Please reveal Yourself to me. Amen."

Instantly, a light bulb went on in his head and he understood everything he had heard. All the Scripture became clear to him and his life drastically changed. He got well, went home, and never looked back. He grew strong in the Word of God. He

THE TRUNK

witnessed to and led others to Christ, including some of his patients when he was practicing medicine.

> *Therefore, if anyone is in Christ, he is a new creation;*
> *old things have passed away;*
> *behold, all things have become new.*
> 2 Corinthians 5:17

Does God guide our lives? Yes, He does, and He cares—down to the number of hairs on our heads. "But the very hairs of your head are all numbered. Do not fear therefore; you are of more value than many sparrows" (Luke 12:7).

Can we trust Him to guide us? Yes! Every day. "I will instruct you and teach you in the way you should go; I will guide you with My eye" (Psalm 32:8).

God continued to guide their lives and lead them on to new places. At forty years of age (my mom was thirty-nine), Dad was exhausted. He was up all night delivering babies, all morning with surgeons in surgery, and all afternoon with patients in his office. He told my mom he couldn't keep this up. In the last month he had delivered twenty-nine babies; that is almost a baby a day! So he sold his medical practice and we moved to Rochester, Minnesota. Then he went to the Mayo Clinic to train in a specialty—one that would give him a normal life and time with his family.

In his last year of residency at the Mayo Clinic, he stood on the street in Rochester and boldly told another doctor (Jack Pasqual) from California that he was planning to move there.

MY FAMILY ROOTS

"You'll never get in!" Jack said. "Well, I'm going to try anyway," my dad said. Everyone wanted to move to California in those days and the state boards were tough. They were not making it easy to start a practice in the Golden State. Dr. Pasqual would later practice in southern California and be the doctor for our youngest son in a time of need.

As my dad left on the train to take his state boards, he read an article in a medical journal on the latest discoveries about leprosy. The state boards were difficult and the doctors interviewing him were not particularly friendly. The first question was, "Since you are a specialist, and think you know so much, tell us all you know about leprosy."

Wow! God had been leading him and had specifically prepared him by reading that article on the train so he could answer them with all the latest on the subject.

The next question, "Tell us all you know about …" and they named a rare disease. He had just had a lecture at the Mayo Clinic on that very disease. He passed his boards. God wanted us to go to California.

It was during the time of his residency, when my dad was forty-three, that I was born. My dad sold our house and moved our family to Pasadena. My two older brothers were eight and twelve, and I was one. They had dreamed of living in a place where flowers grew on the side of the freeway in the middle of winter. They never moved back to Minnesota; they would never shovel snow again!

Dad had his own medical practice in California for the next thirty years until he retired.

Despite all the advancements during their lifetime, and their humble beginnings, the sovereign hand of God was on their lives from beginning to end. Does God guide our lives? Yes! Can we trust Him to guide us? Yes!

After my mom had passed away from Alzheimer's at the age of eighty-five, I was cleaning out a dresser and found an old spiral notebook stuck underneath one of the drawers. I pulled it out and found the story of my parents' lives; it was their testimony. Mom had written it when she realized she was forgetting things. What a treasure that was for me to have their story written down! We made copies and gave it to all of the grandchildren as we celebrated my dad's ninetieth birthday. It told how God had led them and guided them throughout their lives.

My dad's favorite verse at the end of his life was Psalm 37:25, "I have been young, and now am old; yet I have not seen the righteous forsaken, nor his descendants begging bread."

He lived to be ninety-two, full of wisdom and a strong mind. Around the age of eighty-eight, he told me he was memorizing the Psalms. I was so surprised. How he could even memorize at that age was amazing! I asked him why he was doing this. He answered (and I will never forget what he said), "It gives me peace in the night." My mom was in heaven and he missed her, and this made sleeping difficult at times.

How many times when we can't sleep we worry. Things seem worse in the dark and our troubles bigger, our loneliness harder to bear. It is then that those psalms written centuries ago come to mind and give us peace in the night. Try to memorize Scripture. It will pop into your mind when you least expect it and desperately need it. It brings answers to your problems and peace to your soul.

I rejoice at Your word as one who finds great treasure.
Psalm 119:162

2

Mount Hermon: Rats, Ants, and Salvation

*Then you will call upon Me and go and pray to Me, and
I will listen to you. And you will seek Me and find Me,
when you search for Me with all your heart.*
Jeremiah 29:12-13

After living in California a short time, my family took a vacation to Yosemite in Northern California. On the way home we visited a Christian conference center near Santa Cruz, called Mount Hermon, and loved it. They hosted conferences all summer with wonderful speakers at their retreat center right in the middle of the beautiful Redwood forest.

The next summer, my parents bought an old cabin there and spent the next few years fixing it up. What an adventure that was for us! The cabin had its flaws and nuisances, but being at Mount Hermon provided so many opportunities for growth in our young lives that it was invaluable.

We spent the school year in Pasadena, and then Mom and the kids went to Mount Hermon for the summer. Dad spent a few weeks there on and off throughout the summer. I watched my parents sacrifice many times for the sake of their children's walk with the Lord and to give us opportunities; this was one of those sacrifices.

One night I woke up to a lot of noise. My mom, my two brothers, and I were there without my dad. My oldest brother, Jim, was seventeen at the time. I peeked out my window to find the source of the noise. Then I saw Jim down in front of the garage swinging a shovel at a large rat as it circled him. The garage was underneath the house and was full of rats. At night I would hear them gnawing in the walls right next to my bed. I would beat on the wall, and it would be quiet for a little while, but then they would start at it again.

There were lots of adventures with bugs and nature up there in the beautiful mountains. I will never forget the summer I was sick in bed with strep throat. My room was invaded with very large black ants. I pulled my bed away from the wall hoping they wouldn't get on my bed. Another morning my mom was changing Phil's sheets and found a scorpion in his bed. We thanked God that it had not stung my brother. What a great reminder of how faithfully God watches over us!

MOUNT HERMON: RATS, ANTS, AND SALVATION

All of these little trials and inconveniences were great preparation for my life. Little did I know then that I would soon be in Florida with huge spiders, giant cockroaches, and alligators!

Eventually, the cabin was fixed up, the rats moved out, and the ants left.

By the time I was about twelve I started working part-time at the Conference Center. I helped in Daily Vacation Bible School, cleaned cabins, and made beds. One of my fond memories was running the popcorn machine at night. They gave me ten percent of what I sold, so I would get the machine going during the evening meetings, and the fragrance of the popcorn would draw people in afterward.

During all this time I was able to hear great preachers that came to speak at its many conferences held all summer. My mother would take me with her to the evening services to listen. I was saturated with good teaching and countless tools that would equip me for life. One speaker that stands out in my mind's eye was a tall man who wore a white suit. His preaching was powerful and passionate. His name was Alan Redpath. Years later, we met this man again, and God used him in an instrumental and impacting way to change the course of our lives.

Looking back, I can see that God had His hand on my life from the very beginning. He led me to Himself and always provided for us.

THE TRUNK

For this is God, our God forever and ever;
He will be our guide even to death.
Psalm 48:14

One night when I was seven years old, I sat in the second row with Mom. The speaker asked anyone who would like to ask the Lord Jesus to come into their heart to raise their hand.

I knew I wanted to go to heaven, and I did not want to go to hell. I understood what I was doing; it was my age of accountability, and I wanted Jesus. I raised my hand! My mom leaned over and said very seriously, "Honey, you have already received Him." I didn't remember ever doing that, but I knew I wanted Jesus at that moment. Tears ran down my cheeks. My mom realized this was the moment of salvation for me. She didn't say another word but allowed me to settle this in my own soul.

The man on the other side of me leaned over and said, "Don't ever let anyone stop you from coming to Jesus." I had to smile because my mom loved the Lord. She wasn't trying to stop me but perhaps wanted to make sure I knew what I was doing. If you search for God with all your heart, you will find Him, but better than that … He will find you!

That special day in June was my birthday—my spiritual birthday. Jesus knows all things. He knew I would come. He sought me early. I felt His love. That was the night I turned to follow Him. It was the best day of my life! I stepped from hell to heaven, from destruction to salvation. I stepped into a personal relationship with the eternal God, and I would never be the same. I belonged to Him. Although I wouldn't know for a few years that I was to give up my will for His, at this point I learned and wanted to just follow, to belong. A dear friend of mine put it this way: to just "host His presence."

I asked my mother how I would know for sure if I was saved. She said, "When you want others to know Jesus too, it is a sure sign you are born again." I often worried it hadn't taken and perhaps He hadn't come in, so I would ask Him again to make sure. I did want to see others know the love and peace of Jesus, and found rest in that thought.

> *But now, thus says the L*ORD*, who created you,*
> *O Jacob, and He who formed you, O Israel:*
> *"Fear not, for I have redeemed you;*
> *I have called you by your name; you are Mine."*
> Isaiah 43:1

I will never forget those summers at Mount Hermon, hearing God's Word, hearing wonderful speakers, and growing in my faith. I loved the Bible stories so much that my cousin and I would take turns teaching them on flannel-graph boards with my mom as our audience. The Scriptures tell us to train up a child when he is young. I came to Christ when I was very young. No child is too young to hear the things of God and be inspired to know Him more. Don't neglect to tell the little ones about His love and the truths of His Word. Even if you didn't receive a godly heritage, you can pass one on to the next generation.

Chuck Smith's wife, from Calvary Chapel of Costa Mesa, once said that the Hebrew mothers would take their newborn babies in their arms and whisper in their ears, "Jehovah is God." Deuteronomy 6:5-7 says, "You shall love the Lord your God with all your heart, with all your soul, and with all your strength. And these words which I command you today shall be in your heart. You shall teach them diligently to your children, and shall talk of them when you sit in your house, when you walk by the way, when you lie down, and when you rise up."

3

Praying with Childlike Faith

*It shall come to pass that before they call, I will answer;
and while they are still speaking, I will hear.*
Isaiah 65:24

When I was in first grade, I saw someone play the accordion on TV. It fascinated me! I begged my parents for one and began accordion lessons. However, it was very heavy to carry to school. A few years later, I was ready to give it up. The bulky accordion was left at home, and the piano became my musical instrument of choice—that I never had to move!

My piano teacher was a lovely Christian woman. She gave me priceless advice at one of my lessons. She said, "Your husband is alive somewhere on the earth today, and you can pray for him." Wow! I thought I was too young to even think about that. But she said, "Why not?" I thought, *Well, maybe she is right.* So I began to pray for him, not every day, but from time to time. I would pray that God was preparing me for him and him for me—if it was His plan for me to be married.

How fascinating that God hears us pray when we are just little children and answers us! God had plans for my life that I didn't know about, but they were something I could pray about and trust Him to accomplish.

I first met Don, my husband, at youth group in our church in Pasadena. Our mothers were friends and were in a prayer meeting together, though Don and I had never met.

The day I met him, I told my mom I would like to go out with him. Mom said, "Why don't you pray about it?" I said, "He doesn't even know my name."

"That doesn't matter," she said. "God does!"

Call to Me, and I will answer you, and show you great and mighty things, which you do not know.
Jeremiah 33:3

I went to bed and prayed, "Lord, if there is anything to this, let him ask me out. If not, let us not waste our time." I crawled in bed and left it up to God. Then I left for the rest of the summer.

I went to summer school at Westmont College in Santa Barbara, California. When summer school was finished, I took a job at the college painting offices with my friend, Dixie. There is plenty of time to have great conversations when you are painting walls! One day we talked about the question, "How do you know when you're in love?" We had no answers. We decided you could just marry any nice Christian guy that you liked and that was all there was to it; maybe there was no such thing as "falling in love." That was ... until Don asked me out at the end of the summer.

He sat near me in youth group, and we talked ... and talked. He asked if he could drive me over to visit my friend, Margie, who was the pastor's daughter. She had just had her wisdom teeth out. I'll never forget the look on my mom's face as I quickly said, "Mom, Don McClure is giving me a ride home tonight. See you later!"

In three short months we were engaged. One year later, three days before Christmas, we were married in the middle of our senior year of college.

I have been asked by younger women through the years, "How do you know when you're in love?" I have an answer now. "You never want to go out with anyone else again!"

This is the same with our love for the Lord. Like the woman at the well, once we find Him and fall in love with Him, the world loses its interest. We stop looking and searching for love and peace and fulfillment. We have found it in the lovely face of Jesus!

Don and I met at the perfect time. He had come to Christ at a Billy Graham Crusade in Los Angeles two years earlier. That summer he met weekly with ten guys to pray. All of them went on to serve in some kind of ministry. They loved Jesus, and soon Don did too! He had dreamed of being a businessman like his dad and grandfather, and had gotten his Bachelor of Science degree in business administration at Cal Poly. But his heart changed that summer as he fell in love with Jesus and felt called to the ministry. He set his life apart and asked God to bring his wife to him; he was through with dating.

When I was fifteen years old, I too felt called to be in ministry. God was preparing us for each other—step by step, year by year—until we finally met. We were headed down the same road, on the same path.

My life was greatly impacted by the godly advice from my piano teacher and my mom. They encouraged me to pray! God heard my prayers for my husband from the time I was just a child. He hears our prayers; He listens and answers. Tell the young children to pray for their mate when they are young (or if they are called to be single, that God would use them mightily like Paul). God hears and answers the prayers of His children.

4

Boarding School

Everyone comes naked from their mother's womb, and as everyone comes, so they depart. They take nothing from their toil that they can carry in their hands.
Ecclesiastes 5:15 (NIV)

My folks believed in Christian schools and felt strongly that they were an important foundation in the lives of children. So when my brother was old enough to enter high school, they sent him to a Christian boarding school in Orlando, Florida, called Hampden Dubose Academy (HDA). Seven short years later they sent me to the same school where I would remain for the next four years.

My adventure began with a three-day journey across the country by train from Pasadena, California, to Orlando, Florida. I was only fourteen years old when they sent me away to school.

THE TRUNK

Florida was dramatically different from what I was used to or what I expected. I was delighted by the sights of moss hanging from the trees and the tropical weather, and mystified by the huge lakes surrounding the area with alligators swimming in them somewhere. The school property had formerly been an old estate with beautiful large homes and orange groves. To my surprise, I loved it. It was hard not seeing my parents for nine months at a time, but life was busy and fun, so it felt like being at summer camp all year-round.

Many of my classmates' parents were missionaries serving all over the world. It was there that I was first introduced to books by authors like Amy Carmichael and Elisabeth Elliot, who had actually been a teacher at my school before she married Jim Elliot.

We often had four girls sharing a room, sometimes five. Two of Billy Graham's daughters were my roommates. Nate Saint, who had been martyred in Ecuador years earlier, had a daughter who was my "little sister" while there. They would pair up lower classmen and new students with upper classmen for mentorship and discipleship.

One of my best friends had parents who were missionaries to the Pygmies in Africa. She saw her mother only once in four years and did not see her father at all. I admired Marilyn Spees so much. She had such a joy, and she simply trusted God to take care of her. There were others whose parents were great preachers and speakers who were famous in their time and served God with their whole heart.

BOARDING SCHOOL

I was being exposed to those who lived in full-time ministry, to saints and missionaries, to God's people who lived by faith and on a shoestring budget. Even our teachers were serving as missionaries in a sense, not taking a salary and having to raise their own support to even be there. They had hearts for the Lord and wanted to impart their deep faith to their students and required much from us. Some of my teachers required that we memorize whole chapters of Scriptures at a time.

Yes, our school was very strict and had serious rules, but that didn't bother me; my parents had similar rules. My dad sat me down before I left to go to school and said, "Never complain. No matter what they put in front of you, don't complain about it." I found that to be great advice for life, and God has reminded me of it many times through the years. The choice is ours whether we accept with joy what is placed before us or choose to complain. I choose joy!

I was on a great adventure at boarding school, but it was going to take me further and deeper with the Lord than I anticipated—it was going to change the entire direction of my life!

Lolly Sutton was one of my roommates, and although she was two years older, we became close friends. We both had grown up in Southern California and had many things in common. One afternoon as we were jogging on the track for gym class (or PE, as they called it in those days), we had a conversation that I will never forget. She came from a wealthy home, but she was planning on leaving that behind and heading to the mission field after she graduated from college. She felt God had called her to South America when she was a freshman.

As we talked, she asked me if I would be willing to go to the mission field or into full-time Christian service. My answer was "No, not really." I was fourteen years old and I was planning on having fun; going to live in a hut somewhere and eat who-knows-what on the other side of the earth did not appeal to me. My answer was a firm, *No!!!* When my brother Phil was three, he had thought of going to Africa when he grew up. I thought one missionary per family was plenty. I would let Phil take that duty. As it turned out, Phil never went to Africa but he became a public high school teacher to the jungles of Northern California. He loved it and his students loved him.

One year later, when I was a sophomore and fifteen years old (and Lolly was a senior), we were sitting together in a Vespers service when a guest speaker asked if anyone wanted to serve the Lord. He asked specifically if anyone was willing to go to the mission field or willing to serve wherever God would call them. I sat there very uncomfortably, not willing to raise my hand. I became so miserable. I suddenly knew someone was praying for me, and I felt even worse. The feeling became so strong that it felt as if that person were sitting right next to me. I sensed tremendous conviction, and I was fighting it with everything that was in me.

After the meeting was over, I turned to Lolly (who was sitting right next to me) and asked her, "Have you been praying for me?"

"What do you mean?" she innocently answered.

"Have you been praying that I would become a missionary?"

She hesitated to tell me at first, but then she said something I will never forget. She said, "Yes, ever since our conversation last year on the track when you said you could never go into full-time ministry, I began praying for you to be willing to serve the Lord wherever He wanted you to go."

For an entire year this girl, an upper classman, had bothered to pray for me, a lowly freshman ... ONE WHOLE YEAR!

Do I do that for others? Pray and never give up? Do I quietly take them to Jesus when I see needs in their lives? She prayed for an entire year and never said a word. Thank you, Lolly, for not giving up and for loving me enough to bother.

That night, after my roommates fell asleep (all three of them), I got down on my knees beside my bunk and talked to the Lord. I sensed His question in my heart, *Well, what are you going to do with your life?* I thought I could present my case and end all this talk about leaving my homeland for some faraway country.

"Okay, Lord, if I go wherever You want me to go and do what You want me to do, then life could be difficult." I had by this time read several missionary biographies, all of which appeared to be full of sacrifices. "First, if I went to the mission field, let's say India, I would have to give up all of my friends. They would forget about me. And if I went to Africa, I would have to eat monkey heads and live in huts. Secondly, I would probably never marry—no one would want to go with me. And thirdly, I would have to give up my country." (You couldn't get into India in those days as an American.) "Lord, I love my country, and You wouldn't want me to leave all this," I pleaded.

Silence. Then I heard that still, small voice—that grips your heart—say, "Jean, when you were born, what did you have with you?"

"Well, nothing. I didn't bring any friends. I didn't have a purse—no money. I actually didn't even bring clothes." "Everyone comes naked from their mother's womb, and as everyone comes, so they depart. They take nothing from their toil that they can carry in their hands" (Ecclesiastes 5:15, NIV).

"That's right," the Lord said. "And when you die, you will take nothing with you, except your relationship with Me. Now, what would you like to do with the rest of your life?"

Then somehow, at age fifteen, I knew: if I were the wealthiest woman in the world and did not follow the Lord wherever He wanted me to go and whatever He wanted me to do, I would never be truly happy. But, on the other hand, if I was in His will and went wherever He wanted me to go and did whatever He wanted me to do, I would be happy, peaceful, and satisfied.

"Okay, Lord. You win! I will go into full-time Christian work, missionary or not. Lead me. Guide me."

I had taken a giant step of dying to my will. You see, at age seven, I was saved—going to heaven—I had my ticket for that train, but that was all. I needed to learn it was more than that; it was dying to myself, my will, and my plans. I had finally chosen to slip my hand into His and say, "Lead me ... wherever You choose."

So far, it has not been a bad choice. In fact, I wouldn't trade a life of following Jesus for anything in the world—not for a million dollars or a thousand diamonds.

When I look at women as I speak at retreats, I am so grateful that He uses me at all. I stand in awe at the value of each of their souls and the impact God's Word spoken through a weak, yet willing vessel can have on their lives. If one of their souls enters heaven, it is an awesome gift of God. If one of them says, "Not my will, but Thine," it is a great victory. If just one of them goes back and repairs her marriage or gets on her knees for her rebellious child or enters a life of intercessory prayer or finds faith to see that God can do the impossible, I can say, it has been worth it all!

God never called me to full-time service in foreign lands; I became a pastor's wife in America. But by His grace, He has allowed me to spend time abroad to encourage believers and support God's work. He even allowed me to go to India once and I wept as I saw their precious faces—giving up everything for the gospel. In India, to profess faith in Jesus Christ means complete alienation and rejection from your family and country; they lose everything to follow Christ. What an example of sacrifice and devotion! I have also had the privilege to travel to Uganda,

Africa. There I saw the Potter's Field children quietly stand in line for an hour for their one hot meal of the week, grateful and thankful, a couple of them even sharing a plate.

Lolly and her husband, whom she met at Biola University, became missionaries to Columbia. She died in her early thirties of a brain tumor, but the legacy of her life lived on through the impact she made on my life. She was a prayer warrior that God used to change my course. I will always be grateful for the upper classman who bothered to pray for a lowly freshman for twelve months that I would follow the Lord wherever He called me to go.

I wouldn't trade the life of ministry for anything in this world.

5

Learning for Life

*Now faith is the substance of things hoped for,
the evidence of things not seen.*
Hebrews 11:1

Learning to Trust: Basic Lessons for Life

As I recall memories from my trunk, I recognize how profoundly the Lord used those boarding school years to teach me what I would need later on in life; these lessons formed my attitudes and thinking about serving the Lord in ministry. They were necessary instruments in the Master's hand used to train me to live by faith and not by what I could see and feel. "For we walk by faith, not by sight" (2 Corinthians 5:7). My dear friend, Marilyn Spees, who was in my class all four years, illustrated this truth in her daily life. She showed me what living by faith looked like.

THE TRUNK

When we arrived in the fall of our freshman year, the school required us to bring a list of things we would need, from bedding and towels, to the amount and type of clothing necessary for each season. In those days, the southern custom was that you dressed up for dinner and Sunday mornings. The girls were required to wear a dress, complete with nylons, a hat, and gloves. The boys wore slacks and a sport coat to dinner. We wore dresses to class and dinner every night, except for Saturdays when we had campfire night, consisting of hot dogs and hamburgers. Saturday nights were our favorite night of the week.

In all the humidity of Florida, a hair dryer was an essential commodity. Marilyn came from Africa and didn't have one; and with a full head of red hair, she needed one. "God will send me one," she said confidently. She believed the verse that said "your Father knows the things you have need of before you ask Him" (Matthew 6:8). She held on to Scripture and reminded me of a verse that said, "It shall come to pass that before they call, I will answer; and while they are still speaking, I will hear" (Isaiah 65:24). She knew God would meet her needs through His ability alone.

That same week a teacher came with a hairdryer that someone had sent to the school just for Marilyn. I marveled at God's faithful provision and quietly tucked this lesson into the trunk of treasures in my heart.

Another thing we were required to bring to school was a footlocker (a small trunk) to hold all of our things. I learned all about trunks—and all you fit into them—during my childhood.

Each summer, my family would drive eight hours north from Pasadena, California, to Mount Hermon in our big, old station wagon. My mom used an old black trunk and packed it full of all the things we would need for the entire summer.

In a spiritual sense, my trunk holds countless things I need for life. I would say faith was one of the most important treasures I pull out of my trunk from my high school years. Quite frankly, it is never about how big our faith is, but more importantly, it's about getting a glimpse of how big is our God. It was also not about what I thought I needed or wanted, but rather what He knew was important. His daily lessons were personal for my growth and maturity and preparation for my future.

One Sunday morning the Lord helped me put feet to my budding faith when I realized I had about thirty-five cents left to my name. My mom had been very ill recovering from major surgery and had forgotten to send my allowance for the month. My friend Lolly was also low on funds; she had lost the check that her father had sent to her. I walked into her room, which was next to mine, and said, "This is going to be a great day, Lolly. Today I am putting all the money I have into the offering. It will be my best offering ever, like the widow and her two mites" (see Luke 21:1-4).

"Oh," she said, "I was feeling terrible because I didn't have much to put in the offering today."

"No, it's wonderful! We are giving God everything we have!" She began to view the situation differently and a wide smile spread across her face.

THE TRUNK

Another lesson God taught me about money was that it is truly more blessed to give than to receive. As my understanding of this scriptural principle grew, I began to look for ways to give to others. "And remember the words of the Lord Jesus, that He said, 'It is more blessed to give than to receive'" (Acts 20:35).

One of my sweet classmates named Becky was a missionary child whose parents served in Columbia. I noticed her everyday shoes were wearing out and had holes in the bottom of them. An idea popped into my head and I said, "Becky, your shoes are about gone. You know how Marilyn often prays and believes God will provide for her? God always answers those prayers! How about you and I pray and ask God to bring you some new shoes?"

"Okay," she said timidly, and we prayed together.

A couple of weeks later my mom remembered to send my allowance. In a letter she said she had put in extra money this month so I would be able to give something to a missionary student who needed it. Yes, it was the exact amount needed for a new pair of shoes! My mom knew nothing about Becky's need or our prayer. I asked one of the staff to pick up a pair of shoes for me and give them to Becky without telling her where the money came from to buy them.

I will always remember her face when she came running to me across the gym field. "Jean," she called as she ran, "God sent me my new shoes!"

"Oh wow, Becky! That is so great! God answered our prayers." I never told her I was the one who bought them. She didn't need to know. All she knew was that God loved her by providing for her needs.

The staff and teachers at HDA were not paid a salary. They all lived by faith like missionaries, and as money came in to the school, it was dispersed to meet their needs. They had given their lives to teach us and take care of us, and I watched their examples closely. As I began to find the joy in giving, I sometimes left envelopes with a little cash in them at their places at dinner. Sad to say, I didn't do this as often as I probably should have.

One evening at dinner, a teacher sitting next to me told me how God had provided for her through a gift of money at the table; it was exactly what she needed. I never said a word about my gift to her, but treasured in my heart the thrill of being an instrument of God's blessing to her in her need.

I was so young, and yet I was daily learning such valuable lessons that would impact my life forever—more treasures in my trunk. Never think your children are too young to learn the principles of Scripture, to hear God's message, or know His call on their lives.

Sometimes our gifts are not financial, but words of kindness given. A couple of days ago, I asked my daughter-in-law, Brenda, what she was doing for her son Joshua's birthday. She told me that for all of the kids' birthdays (they have six kids), she prepares a special tea breakfast. During breakfast, they go around the table and each person shares some wonderful quality they see in the birthday person. *How absolutely lovely,* I thought. They would grow up feeling loved and appreciated by their siblings, and on rough days when they weren't getting along, they would remember the kind word a brother or sister said about them. Such a lovely tradition my grandchildren are putting in to their own trunks.

Devotional Life

One evening we were enjoying a meal in the dining room at school; it was a lovely setting with linen table cloths, soft music playing in the background, and crystal chandeliers sparkling overhead. I asked the boy sitting next to me, "How is it that some people get saved and never change, never grow? In fact, it's hard to even know they are a Christian?" I was bothered by the question of how can you truly know Christ and walk away from Him.

"It is simple," said the young fellow student. "The ones who grow have a devotional time—time spent in the Word and in prayer. The ones who don't grow and go on with the Lord simply don't!" Later I read the parable of the sower in Luke's gospel, and Jesus explained this principle beautifully (see Luke 8:5-15). The seed needs to be watered and nourished or it remains stagnant or it dies; it must not be choked out by the things of this world, the lusts of the world, the pride of life.

I have found this to be one of my most valuable lessons from those days in high school. It has caused me to dig deeper when the storms are greatest. I am a student of the Word because

I have seen firsthand the value of it and the life-changing power in reading it. God's Word has strengthened me when I was weak, given me hope when there was none from my perspective, and answered my questions when I have struggled in the dark. His Word has truly preserved my soul.

I eagerly look forward to waking up in the morning and sitting down with a steaming cup of coffee as I open God's Word to see what He has to say to me each day. It is exciting to see the answers that are found in the pages of Scripture. The older I get, the earlier I wake up. He wakes me early when it is still dark. I love it! "He wakens me morning by morning, wakens my ear to listen like one being instructed" (Isaiah 50:4, NIV).

The greatest lessons from boarding school were these: First, my devotional life was going to be the key foundation to everything I would encounter on this journey called life; it would give me hope. Second, God was sufficient for everything I would need. He would take care of me no matter what the need or what the cost. You see, my Father owns the cattle on a thousand hills (Psalm 50:10). Sometimes He just has to sell one for me! I know He will never leave me nor forsake me. "When my father and my mother forsake me, then the LORD will take care of me" (Psalm 27:10). Although my parents didn't forsake me, they sent me to boarding school on the other side of the country where I had to live apart from them for all four years of high school, only coming home in the summer. This hardship forged my trust in God as my heavenly Father and caused me to lean into

Him more. Third, nothing is impossible for Him. Fourth, He would lead and guide me every single day of my life and in every circumstance—if I would simply look to Him.

Revelation 3:8 became my life verse. It says, "I know your works. See, I have set before you an open door, and no one can shut it; for you have a little strength, have kept My word, and have not denied My name." He would lead me through open doors that He had placed before me and guide my life if I kept His Word. Did this mean life would be perfect and easy—just like that Norman Rockwell painting in my mind's eye? Absolutely not. I have often dreamed about an easy, picture-perfect life, but that isn't reality. It is the storms in life that cause my roots to go down deeper, allow character to develop, and allow me to know God in greater ways—so for them I will be grateful.

6

Capernwray, England

And the L<small>ORD</small>*, He is the One who goes before you. He will be with you, He will not leave you nor forsake you; do not fear nor be dismayed.*
Deuteronomy 31:8

We had a lovely Christmas wedding in December of 1968. All white with red poinsettias. I borrowed Jenny's (my sweet sister-in-law) beautiful dress that was white satin and fit me like a glove. We ate red velvet cake with white frosting at the reception at the University Club. It was a picture-perfect start to our life together.

We rented a little apartment and finished college in the spring. I dreamed we would live happily ever after—just like the fairy tales we all grew up with in the '60s. I gazed at Norman Rockwell paintings (being an art minor in school, they fascinated me), and could imagine such a wonderful life: home, family—

the great American dream! I wanted this Norman Rockwell life because it seemed to be perfect. But real life isn't like that. Our plans and ideas are not always God's. And I would learn that His ways are far, far better for us, but will not always be easy or exactly what we would choose for ourselves. "For My thoughts are not your thoughts" (Isaiah 55:8).

> *Oh, the depth of the riches both of the wisdom*
> *and knowledge of God! How unsearchable are His*
> *judgments and His ways past finding out!*
> Romans 11:33

A man named Alan Redpath came into our lives at the time and invited us to go to Bible school at Capernwray in England. He had pastored Moody Church for nine years, as well as large churches in London and Scotland. At this point in his life, he had retired from being a senior pastor to travel around the world and preach the gospel. He was a guest speaker at our church. God sent him to us at just the right time.

Our pastor discouraged us from going to England. He told us that if we went to England, Don would not be hired by that church when we returned. Only our mothers supported us going at first; eventually, our dads supported us as well. In fact, my dad bought us round-trip tickets on a charter flight, just to make sure we'd be safe and to assure that we would come home in nine months.

I had wanted to go to Capernwray since high school. I let that thought go because of the need to finish college, and then because I was married. But that desire was God's desire! Isn't it funny how God puts desires into your heart and then fulfills those desires years later.

It was a year that would change us so much. Don grew in the depth and knowledge of the Word. He learned he would never be perfect or good enough; he didn't need to because God was all that for us. He learned the importance and necessity of dying to yourself, your will, and your works, and letting God take control.

And I ... I began to learn how this marriage thing worked. I too needed to die to myself and trust God through Don. I never realized how selfish I could be until I had to follow someone else. We were both growing up. We both had to trust God for His leading.

We sold our cars and stored our wedding gifts to go to England, but had very little money left over after we paid our tuition. We somehow got through. For Christmas break we went to Scotland to stay with a lovely young couple who were close friends with the Redpaths.

We walked the streets of Edinburgh and loved every minute of it. Don looked up his Scottish plaid and told the shopkeeper he was Scotch. The man said, "No, you're not!" Don said, "Yes, I am—McClure is Scotch." After an argument this man said, "You can be Scottish, or a Scott, but if you are Scotch you'd be in a bottle!" He was right!

For Easter break we wanted to go to Switzerland to L'Abri (Francis Schaeffer's school). But we needed an extra $200 to get there and back on the train. I prayed, "Lord, You know we need

THE TRUNK

$200 if we are to go. It's up to You to supply it, if it's Your will." That week a check came in the mail from my husband's sister, Marilyn, from a small investment we had made in a business that was sold. The check was for $200. Again and again God showed us His faithful provision.

The weather was freezing cold in the north of England. It was so damp and cold that I wore several layers of clothes—including Don's socks—as well as Bermuda shorts under my skirt. Don told people I was ninety pounds, and the rest was just clothes. I was a bit homesick, but our hearts were warmed and sustained by the things God was teaching us.

The night before we left, some of the guys at the school planned to throw Don into a frozen shallow pond. He was such a prankster that they decided to get him good. I was packing and Don was out running from our fellow classmates! Finally, they caught him and held him over the frozen pond. He was yelling as loudly as he could for our school principal (Stuart Briscoe, who is now a well-known speaker and dear friend, with Jill, his dear wife).

"Stuart," he yelled, "What kind of a principal are you? I need help!"

Just then they dropped Don to the ground and disappeared. Don looked up and there stood Stuart in his pajamas staring down at him.

"Mr. McClure," he said, and I am sure he was smiling all the way back to his house thinking, *Those crazy Americans!*

How like the Lord that scene was—although it was fun. In life we find ourselves held and threatened over frozen ponds, fearing we will be dropped in. The Lord comes just at the right moment. He will rescue us. He will see us through. He will be there. He will not fail us, nor give us more than we can bear.

Sometimes we just need more perspective when we're in the thick of it. I often tell myself, *This won't matter in a hundred years.* (I love one-liners, and I often make them up because they are easy to remember and apply to life!) Often that awful thing we feared was going to happen doesn't even matter the next day. And in a hundred years, I shall be in heaven and it certainly won't matter then, for it will be clear as to why God led us through the things He did.

7

Provision to the Penny

*And my God shall supply all your need according to
His riches in glory by Christ Jesus.*
Philippians 4:19

Our time in England had come to a close. What a treasured time that was for us and for our walks with the Lord! We left on a train for London and Heathrow Airport. We had a charter flight to catch from the tickets our parents had given us, and so we started our journey home. By this time, I was pregnant with our first child and getting sick several times a day. So I was not up to snuff, as they say, and did not feel like traveling.

As we traveled down to London on the train, Don realized that he had left our passports in the safe at Capernwray. He took me to a Bed and Breakfast near Heathrow and I went to bed. He returned to London on the train and waited for our passports to be hand-delivered. He had called the school and they were sending them by way of the conductor; it was truly "special delivery."

He looked exhausted in the morning when he came for me. We boarded the plane and headed for home. The plane was so heavy from all of the students and their luggage going home that we seemed to sag in mid-air as we took off.

As we flew over the Atlantic Ocean, I slept through the dark night, and Don prayed. He hadn't told me, but he was worried about how we were going to get home. Our plane was landing at the Oakland airport in the San Francisco area. However, we didn't have a ticket to Los Angeles International Airport (which was close to home for us). The other problem was that Don had only $20 left in his pocket.

A pregnant wife, no money, and no way home!

"Lord," he prayed, "I need some help here. We need a ride from Oakland to Los Angeles."

He didn't tell me how bad things were. He let me sleep, and went to Jesus with his problems. Needless to say, he didn't get much rest that flight, but God was at work through it all.

The next day we landed in Oakland. In those days (the early '70s), you would exit the plane down stairs that led directly on to the airstrip to the gate. The "gate" was literally a gate in a chain-link fence. As we walked toward the fence, to our astonishment, we saw Don's parents waiting for us on the other side. What joy and relief flooded our hearts! They said they decided to drive up the coast (almost an eight-hour drive) to pick us up because they hadn't seen us in nine months. They graciously said that they would understand if we would rather take a flight home instead of the long drive.

Isn't God amazing?! We were more than thrilled to get in their car, head for a delicious, juicy American hamburger, and a wonderfully clean bed in a hotel—their treat—and then ride home with them. Two parents never looked so good to a travel-weary, hungry, desperate young couple.

They didn't know we didn't have a flight home, or that I was pregnant and feeling so ill, or that we only had $20 in our wallet.

Don didn't call our parents or ask someone else for help when we needed it. He went to God expectantly, putting all his trust in God, and God in His great faithfulness met us there.

… but God.

8

Children—Firstborn

The firstborn of your sons you shall give to Me.
Exodus 22:29b

Give me your firstborn—

What happens to a child you don't give to the Lord when He asks you?

After our learning season in England, we arrived in Southern California where all of our extended family lived. Apparently, I looked pretty thin for being three months pregnant at a slight 106 pounds. It had not been an easy pregnancy. I threw up about five times a day in the first three months of that pregnancy while we were in England. So my mom, who had been a nurse, took it upon herself to fatten me up. She cooked and I ate—so much so that I gained almost forty-five pounds in the next five months. It was so good to be home!

THE TRUNK

Although I was feeling better and had gained some weight, the doctor was still concerned and ordered bed rest twice for fear that I would lose the child. I had started contractions much too early. The doctor said, "You are only six months along, and the baby won't make it. Off to bed you go." He required the bed rest for two weeks at two different times.

But God wanted the child to live—we both made it to full term. Our precious firstborn, Marcus, was born. He weighed a healthy nine and a half pounds! After a rough pregnancy, the delivery was equally challenging, and the recovery was just as difficult and slow. No one had ever told me that being pregnant and having a baby could be hard. For some girls it may be easy, but for me it was not! I had to stay in the hospital for five days after he was born, and then we went to my mother-in-law's for two weeks before we could even go home.

I shall never forget his first cry. I was thrilled and amazed at how this could even be. How could someone have a baby and not believe there is a God! I certainly couldn't have come up with this idea on my own or possibly breathed life into another human being and made them live. Physically, I felt like a truck had driven over me, but my soul was thrilled down to my toes with this precious new baby. I had almost lost him twice during the pregnancy and had a very hard time at the delivery, but he was a fat and healthy baby! No wonder it was a difficult delivery. He didn't have wrists; he was so plump, he had creases. I decided he was made out of Christmas candy from all I had eaten during the holidays. The sacrifices and struggles were worth it all.

CHILDREN—FIRSTBORN

I still remember that first night: I was alone in my hospital room. Marcus had been taken to the nursery, the relatives were gone, and Don had gone home to get some rest. It was dark and quiet in my hospital room. As I rested there thinking about this amazing gift of life, I became keenly aware of the presence of God.

Then, out of nowhere, I heard Him whisper, "Give me that baby."

In one short sentence, I was at full attention. I thought I would discuss this: "Lord, if I give You this child, You could take him to heaven right now." The process that led to his birth was so hard and so full of surrender and sacrifices already, I felt that there was no way I could bear to lose him now; it was so much work having him.

In my mind, I began to picture the life of a child that had never been given to God, one who had never known Him—void, dark, tragic, even prison—a nightmare. What would a person's life be like if God asked for it and it was not offered but held back in fear? I shuddered inside.

"All right, Lord. He is Yours. I give him to You. I will trust You with his life." Then immediately, peace flooded my heart and mind.

Like Abraham with Isaac, God knew He was asking me for my most prized possession to be placed on the altar of my life.

And like Abraham and Isaac, God gave him back. He did not let him die; it was a test.

THE TRUNK

Through the years—especially the teenage years—I reminded God of this on several occasions. "He is Yours, Lord. Remember, I gave him to You? Teach him. Chase him. Keep him. I gave him to You on his first night. He is Your responsibility."

I must add that although our firstborn son was a rascal and rebellious many times, he has always known and believed in God. He came to the Lord at an early age. I took him to a vacation Bible school at a little pentecostal church in Lake Arrowhead. He practically ran forward twice, fearing hell and wanting heaven.

Much later I read in the Old Testament that God commanded Israel to give their firstborn to Him. I have subsequently given my other two sons to the Lord as well. There is no way we could have done this child-rearing thing on our own. I would learn this lesson many times throughout the years to come, and I'm still learning it.

One day when Marcus was about ten years old, he had gone to school shortly before Don left for work. As Don headed out the door, he felt a strong tug from the Lord to go find Marcus—that he was in trouble. It seemed odd, but Don couldn't get the thought out of his head. He started driving down the road that Marcus would have taken to school. He looked everywhere but didn't see him. He stopped at 7-Eleven and just sat in his car and prayed, thinking, *Where is he?* Then he saw him, somewhat hidden from view by some bushes, smoking a cigarette with his friends. He caught Marcus' eye—busted!

"Get in the car," Don said. He drove him straight to school as they had a father-son chat.

How wonderful that God knows just where our children are and exactly what they are doing! Sometimes He even sends us after them. Marcus often wondered how in the world he would get caught when he was into mischief. We never told him; he would find out and understand when he was a parent.

What is our job as a parent? To pray for them, to give them to the Lord, and raise them to the best of our ability according to God's Word. Each child has their own personality: Some are easy. Some are rebels. Some are compliant. Some walk the line. Some the edge. But no matter what God might have entrusted you with, know that He knows them better than you do. He loves them more than you could ever love them, and He sees them every hour of every day. Our God neither slumbers nor sleeps. God always sees them and knows what they are doing.

School was not Marcus' favorite place to go. He had a high IQ but struggled with dyslexia, which made school more of a social event than anything for him. He was a leader, and where he went, others seemed to follow. He was very fun and very entertaining. When he was in junior high, his teacher was a bit exasperated one day and told me, "When Marcus has a good day, we all have a good day. When Marcus isn't having a good day, I might as well not show up to teach!" He had influence.

One day when he was in grade school, I was doing dishes at the kitchen sink worried about him, and I remember praying,

THE TRUNK

"Lord, are You with him? Do you go to the public school? I hope You're watching over him." Not long after that, the Lord sweetly confirmed to me His presence in the public school. I had the opportunity at a parent/teacher conference to speak with Marcus' teacher, who was not a Christian but knew I was. He took a piece of paper and slid it across the desk in front of me and said he thought I would appreciate seeing his work. It was an assignment from another class where the students were asked to write an essay on their best friend. Marcus had written, "My best friend is Jesus Christ, and I love Him because He died for me." At the top of the paper, the young female teacher had written an A- and underneath she wrote, "He is my best friend too, Marcus." My heart soared. *Thank You, Lord, for clearly showing me that You are in the public school too. You go everywhere with my child!*

9

The Jesus People Movement

But Jesus looked at them and said to them, "With men this is impossible, but with God all things are possible."
Matthew 19:26

Everywhere I looked people in bell-bottom jeans with long hair sat cross-legged on the grassy hills. They weren't in any hurry as they sat around waiting for the concert to begin. It was a crisp, yet sunny spring day in 1971 when we went to a park to hear a group called Love Song. Don's sister, Marilyn, had invited us, thinking we would enjoy this new style of music and new expression of people who loved Jesus. The church that put it on was Calvary Chapel of Costa Mesa, and little did we know, but we were in the early onset of a revival that was later called the Jesus People Movement. What a thrilling time it was!

Our hearts resonated with the style and message of the concert, so we decided to visit Calvary Chapel one Sunday. As we were leaving church that day, the pastor, Chuck Smith, shook Don's hand and greeted him by name. Don was perplexed that Chuck knew his name. Don said, "Excuse me? I don't think we have ever met." Chuck said, "Oh, I'm sorry. Aren't you Don McClure, the one with the Bible study in Hollywood? Some people from your Bible study group have been attending church here and told me about you."

Not long after, Chuck and his wife, Kay, invited us out to lunch to get to know us better. As we talked, Chuck asked Don to share his testimony of how he came to faith in Christ and where God was leading him. At the time, Don had been attending Talbot Theological Seminary and also serving as a youth pastor at Grace Brethren Church in Cypress. (His salary was only $50 a month! Can you imagine?! He painted houses to keep us afloat.) He knew God had called him to ministry and was seeking His will and direction for our lives.

Don visited Calvary Chapel next on a Wednesday night. He sat way in the back to quietly observe the church and see what it was all about. The Word was taught and one could sense the presence of the Lord there. As the service began, Chuck got up and said to everyone, "Don McClure is here with us tonight and … Don, would you come up front and share with us what the Lord has put on your heart?" Don was pretty surprised, but he quickly came up with something to share.

We went to their family camp that summer; it was packed out. On the first night, Chuck got up and announced that Don

McClure would be teaching the following morning. Don was completely taken off guard and not prepared at all. So he stayed up all night to work on his message.

Not long after summer camp, Don went in to the church office for prayer one day. Pastor Romaine and the secretary, Jean Smith, laid hands on him and prayed that he would receive the baptism of the Holy Spirit. He later told me that their hands felt like hot waffle irons on his back while they prayed. He was different afterward, and his sermons came to him more easily.

Don was halfway through his education at Talbot Theological Seminary at the time, and the school did not acknowledge certain gifts of the Holy Spirit, or the baptism of the Holy Spirit. So they told him they would allow him to graduate, but would never place him in a church. Chuck heard about the situation and invited him to come on staff at Calvary Chapel of Costa Mesa; his answer was *yes*. So God placed us right in the church of His choice, and we are so grateful. It was a privilege to be part of the Jesus People Movement.

Those were truly wonderful days! The church was exploding as hundreds of young people and hippies came to faith in Christ. The young people brought their parents with them, and they came to know Jesus also. Within a year, the church had outgrown the little chapel where they met and a new sanctuary was needed to accommodate the crowds that gathered almost every night of the week. A huge white circus tent was erected on a simple dirt lot to hold the services in while a sanctuary was built. That simple tent is now an iconic memory of those early years of the Jesus People Movement. Lives were forever changed as God's Spirit was poured out on His people.

Our mentor and dear friend, Alan Redpath, was speaking in Los Angeles during this season and came to stay with us. We wanted him to see the exciting things God was doing here but wondered if it might be too much for a proper Englishman to handle. So we brought him with us to a Saturday night concert at Calvary Chapel. We stood in the back of the tent filled with hundreds of young people crowded together singing and worshiping the Lord with one voice. As the volume rose, we thought Alan would be anxious to leave, but he surprised us by wanting to linger. When we got into our car, Alan excitedly said, "Did you see those young people? Every one of them had a Bible." Then he added, *"I have waited all my life to see that!"* Here was a man who had been in the ministry for many years—he had pastored a large church in London, a large church in Edinburgh, Scotland, and Moody Church in Chicago for nine years—and he had just seen revival for the first time in America. A treasure of a lifetime!

The church grew at an enormous rate as young people poured in to hear the Word of God taught. We made wonderful friends during those early days of serving at Calvary Chapel of Costa Mesa. I can't even express the feeling of those days. There was a palpable thrill in going to church and attending Bible studies. The revival spanned the generations; young and old were being touched by the Holy Spirit. Even our dads became a part of the work God was doing; they both served faithfully for many years on the church's board of elders.

Miracles were happening all around us—more than I have room to tell in this little book! One time, Don and Romaine (one of the assistant pastors) went to pray for a man who was blind, and he miraculously received his sight. Another time, we were awakened in the night by a phone call from Mike MacIntosh (another one of the assistant pastors). He needed Don to go to the hospital. There had been a terrible accident on the freeway and a man was in a coma being kept alive by machines. When Don arrived, the man's girlfriend was there by his side. This couple had twins together, and the man owned a couple of bars. Don had the privilege of praying with the girlfriend to receive Christ that night and continued to visit the man while he was in the coma. Eventually, Don lost track of him when they moved him to a Veterans' hospital. Almost a year later, Don received a phone call from this man. Miraculously, he began to recover, and when he had regained consciousness, his girlfriend led him to Christ. He was now walking with the Lord, and they wanted to get married. God, in His mercy, was doing miracles like this one everywhere. Hearts and lives were being radically changed by God. It was a great privilege and gift from God to have been there.

He was even doing miracles in our own family. My dad desperately wanted to see a miracle, so he asked the Lord to allow him to personally witness one. Being a doctor, he wanted to put his hands on one before and after, and see it for himself to know it was a miracle. About three months later, my dad developed a lump in his right arm that was the size of a golf ball. A biopsy revealed that it was a very nasty, fast-growing kind of cancer (I can't remember the name of it today). The biopsy results came back on Friday and they planned to operate on his arm the following Monday. During that long weekend of waiting, he came out to see us, and both Don and Chuck prayed for him.

On Monday, the tumor was removed as planned. They were relieved to find that it had not gone into his nerves or bone, which would enable him to continue to use his hands for surgeries and thus continue to practice medicine. The very next day the surgeon, who was my dad's friend, walked into his hospital room with a confused look on his face. He said, "I don't know exactly how to tell you this, Phil. We have the biopsy from Friday which is full of cancer, but when we took out the tumor and had it biopsied yesterday, we did not find a trace of cancer in it; it was completely benign." This kind of thing never happened; it was a medical impossibility.

"Praise God!" my dad said. "It's my miracle!" God had answered his heart's desire to see a miracle firsthand, literally! My dad loved to use this story as an opportunity to share his faith. When people saw the scar on my dad's arm, he would tell them about his miracle, and many believed because he was a medical doctor.

One night at church, Chuck saw him in the audience and knew the amazing miracle God had done with his cancerous tumor. He spontaneously announced that Phil Anderson was going to come up and share his testimony. Though my dad was completely taken off guard at first, it didn't stop him from coming up and sharing. He was thrilled with what God had done and wanted to give Him all the glory.

We serve the God of the impossible. In Jeremiah 32:27 He says, "Is there anything too hard for Me?" We need to take God at His Word and believe His promises. The Jesus People Movement was an amazing time, and we can rejoice in the past, but also trust Him for the present. Jesus is the same yesterday, today, and forever (Hebrews 13:8). We serve an awesome God!

10

Michael's Miracles and the Crippled Children's Society

Therefore God also has highly exalted Him and given Him the name which is above every name.
Philippians 2:9

Life was anything but boring during our first three years at Calvary Chapel of Costa Mesa. We had just moved into our own home across the street from my parents' home in Costa Mesa. Our second son, Michael, who incidentally was born on his brother's birthday—at the exact same minute, three years later—was now eighteen months old. We were having some health concerns about him and were beginning to think we needed a doctor's advice. Over a period of about three months, Michael had not gained weight and was having signs of food allergies, or so we thought. I took him to the pediatrician and told him there was something wrong with my baby. He couldn't figure out what was wrong and wanted us to wait and bring him back again later. He didn't seem too concerned.

One night, Don and I had my parents babysit Marcus and Michael while we went out for dinner. When we came to pick them up, my dad said, "Michael is bleeding in his intestines, and you need to take him to the doctor first thing in the morning." Then he said, "You know, oftentimes someone can have a hole in their intestines and the doctors never find where it is." My dad was extremely concerned.

Our pediatrician was young and kind, but what he had to say that next day was frightening: "I want you to take Michael to the children's hospital, and we are going to admit him. We need to run some tests to determine what is wrong with him. You need to prepare yourselves for the fact that this could possibly be leukemia." On my way home from the doctor's office, I stopped in at Calvary Chapel and told Pastor Chuck. He graciously took the time to come out to the car and pray over Michael. There he sat, asleep in his car seat in his little blue pajamas, so pale and thin. I was beyond worried as I headed home to tell Don and my parents; I dreaded telling them, especially Don. I have rarely seen my husband cry, but that day he wept so hard he could hardly talk. As we sat in the car that afternoon in the parking lot of Children's Hospital in Orange, Don prayed for Michael. "Please,

God, give us back our boy." God walked with us as we stepped into this frightening situation. The young doctor in charge was a Christian and went to our church. What a comfort that was to us! He gathered the medical personnel assigned to Michael into a room with us, and then he had us all stop to pray for Michael before moving forward. At church on Sunday, Chuck led the whole congregation in prayer for Michael.

Once he was admitted to the hospital, they felt he was so weak and sick that he needed a blood transfusion; they gave him so much blood that he turned bright pink. It broke my heart to leave him in that little crib in the hospital overnight. He was so quiet and sweet ... and sick. Then, as quickly as all this had begun, the bleeding stopped. Michael began to get well. We knew that the Lord had touched him. The only thing they could trace back to having caused the bleeding was that I had given Michael an aspirin a few days before because he was catching a cold. They assume he hadn't chewed it properly and that it possibly sat on his intestines and ate a hole right through them. But, of course, that didn't explain the months of prior weakness and sickness. The Lord had healed his little insides, and we were able to bring him home. What a miracle!

Later that week we were visiting with Marilyn, my sister-in-law. As we sat in the kitchen, she asked about Michael's medical bill. It was a pretty hefty sum and Don was only making about $75 a week at that time. "How are you ever going to pay those bills?" she asked. "We don't know," we said. Literally, as we were discussing the impossibility of the situation, the phone rang right next to me. Startled, I picked it up and listened as a voice on the other end said, "Hi. This is the Crippled Children's Society. Do you have a son named Michael McClure? We understand that your son has just been in the hospital for treatment. His story was brought to our attention, and we would like to cover your entire bill."

Wow! Financial provision for needs that we weren't able to meet was another miracle God did to show us firsthand His power and faithfulness. We never found out how they even heard about us. But God knew! The very moment we were wondering what to do and how we would pay for it, God gave us our answer. Isn't our God amazing?

And my God shall supply all your need
according to His riches in glory by Christ Jesus.
Now to our God and Father be glory forever and ever.
Philippians 4:19, 20

Up until this time Michael had not been able to walk. At eighteen months old, he stood and tried to walk, but because he was so weak, he would just sit back down. After the Lord had touched him, everything changed. We brought him home from the hospital and he gained weight and strength, and soon after my dad taught him how to run! How thankful and happy we were to see this transformation. It is interesting to see how full circle God brought his healing; during Michael's first year in college he got a scholarship to run on the cross-country team.

God had made him a runner. He ran through high school and college, and today he still runs with his wife for fitness.

Only weeks after Michael was well and learning to run, Don was asked by Chuck Smith to go to Lake Arrowhead to start a church and a Bible College (which is now in Murrieta). We found a house to buy that was built by the high school in Lake Arrowhead. When I was in high school we built jewelry boxes, not houses; here the students actually learned to build a house as part of their education. Amazing.

One day, Michael and I were out running errands. We were getting ready to move to Lake Arrowhead, and I was picking out paint colors for our new mountain house, and finding things to decorate and add my own touches. We stopped in at the bank where they gave a sucker to Michael, and off we went to Standard Brands, a paint store. Michael was in the shopping cart as we were going through the aisles when suddenly he began to gasp for air; he couldn't breathe. He was choking! I instinctively stuck my finger down his throat to see what it was and there was a big piece of sucker stuck down so far that I could barely touch it. I squeezed his little ribs trying to get him to cough it up—but nothing changed. A crowd began to gather around us as I tried to save my son. One women cried out, "Oh no! He's not breathing." In a panic, the clerk dialed 911. I remember thinking, *Have we just made it through all that we went through with Michael at the Children's Hospital only to lose him in Standard Brands!?*

Just then a man stepped out of the crowd toward me and took Michael into his arms, and before I could say a word, he flipped him upside-down, hanging him by his legs. Still nothing. Michael was turning beet red. My knees were shaking in my bell-bottom jeans as I looked on in horror not being able to do anything. I took his little face in my hands, not caring who in that crowd heard me, and said, "Jesus, touch my baby!" Miraculously, while he was still hanging upside-down, the sucker slipped down—or actually, it slipped up—into his stomach. He immediately took a big gasp of air. He was breathing again! The paramedics arrived just then and rushed into the store. The sucker had sliced his throat and caused him to spit up blood. So, of course, they sent us to our pediatrician to make sure everything was okay. He examined Michael and determined that he was just fine—but I was a wreck. The doctor looked at Michael and said, "You have to stop doing this to your mother."

Some years later I shared this story at a retreat and told the ladies of the power of simply calling on the name of Jesus. When Michael was choking and I called on the name of Jesus, immediately—at the very moment I called His name—the miracle happened. Afterward a woman came up and told me her story: She was driving on the freeway in California with several other ladies in the car when the eighteen-wheeler in front of her suddenly stopped. She knew there was no way she could stop her car in time, and in those days, trucks didn't have the bar at the bottom rear to prevent you from going underneath. She knew they were headed straight under the truck and feared their lives would surely be lost. As she cried out the name of Jesus—just said His name—immediately her engine died and her car stopped short of the truck.

There is power in the name of Jesus! His name encompasses who He is and His very presence when we call upon Him. His name is not just a word; it is not just the name of a person. There is power in His name. Are you in trouble today? Are you hurting? Never be afraid to call out on the name of Jesus. Sometimes He is our only answer—but He is enough. "Therefore God also has highly exalted Him and given Him the name which is above every name" (Philippians 2:9).

11

Our Mountaintop Season in Lake Arrowhead

"For my thoughts are not your thoughts, neither are your ways my ways," saith the LORD. *"For as the heavens are higher than the earth, so are my ways higher than your ways, and my thoughts than your thoughts."*
Isaiah 55:8-9 (KJV)

In the early to mid '70s, Don was an assistant pastor at Calvary Chapel of Costa Mesa and had been serving there for about four years. It was an incredible season in life for us. We had just witnessed an amazing outpouring of God's Spirit during the revival of the Jesus People Movement. The church was growing by the thousands and thriving, and we were happily settling into a routine as a family. I was so happy with our lives. We had bought our first home near the church and my parents moved in across the street. Don's folks had moved down near the beach, which was close to us as well. We had wonderful friends, and the ministry was a delight. Everything was perfect—that Norman Rockwell life I had dreamed about. But as has often been the case for our family, God had different plans and would move us forward in a new direction.

One day a friend of Don's, Bert Smith, took him up to Twin Peaks near Lake Arrowhead in the San Bernardino Mountains of Southern California to show him a beautiful piece of property. The land was built out into a conference center, complete with accommodations, meeting facilities, and a dining hall, and had been owned by the teacher's association. Don was surprised to see the dining room full of dirty dishes and plates left all over the tables. The teacher's association had a dinner party and walked out, leaving the place deserted and a mess, and now it was owned by the bank.

Don went to Chuck Smith with news of this beautiful property and told him he should buy it. Chuck went up with the church elders to see it and got excited about its potential as he remembered his own youth and how God had used his times at camp to impact his life so greatly. Shortly thereafter, Calvary bought what is now known as the Calvary Chapel Conference Center in Twin Peaks. Chuck asked Don if he would move to the mountains to start a Bible College and a church on the property. Don was excited, but I was not excited at all.

We found out later that a small group of Christians had come on the property after the foreclosure and prayed that a

Christian organization would buy it; they prayed it would be used by the Lord.

A couple years earlier, I had asked Kay (Chuck Smith's wife) if she would start a ladies' Bible study in our home. I wanted to learn from her; I wanted to love the Word and prayer like she did. I just wanted to sit at her feet. She graciously said she would ask Chuck and pray about whether God wanted her to do it. Cheryl, her youngest daughter, was still in high school at that time, so that was a consideration for her as well. I begged God to tell her to come. She came to me and told me the Lord had given her the verses from Titus 2:3-5 about older women teaching and admonishing the younger women. "I want you to know I'm not old," she said with a smile, "but I am older than the rest of you." She was in her early forties at the time and we were all in our twenties. What a delight to have her pour into our lives! She had a way of lovingly exhorting us like a passionate mother that we all respected and loved.

I learned so much in those early days from Kay's study. We sat all over my living room, many on the floor, and soaked in like sponges all she taught us. We learned we were to love our husbands and not be critical of them. We learned to love prayer and the Word of God, and we learned to love each other. The study grew so big that the city forced us to move it out of my house. They told me the garbage trucks couldn't get around the cars to pick up the trash. So we had to move our meeting to the church, which was only a few blocks away.

THE TRUNK

At one of the last studies at my house with Kay, I counted seventy ladies. I remember exactly where I was sitting that day because the Lord suddenly, in the midst of the lesson, spoke to my heart. "Will you go to the mountains?" He said gently.

Oh, Lord, please don't ask me to do that. My parents just moved in across the street. I love it here. Marcus would walk over to their house in the morning and have breakfast with them—such a sweet time. I have found that those perfect days rarely last forever, so enjoy them while you can and be thankful for them.

That night the Lord spoke to me out of the book of Isaiah. Looking back I have seen that when God called Don and me to something new, He impressed it strongly on Don's heart and afterwards gave me a Scripture verse confirming it; often the verses described the places we were actually moving to.

> *"For my thoughts are not your thoughts, neither are your ways my ways," saith the* LORD. *"For as the heavens are higher than the earth, so are my ways higher than your ways, and my thoughts than your thoughts. For as the rain cometh down, and the snow from heaven, and returneth not thither, but watereth the earth, and maketh it bring forth and bud, that it may give seed to the sower, and bread to the eater: So shall my word be that goeth forth out of my mouth: it shall not return unto me void, but it shall accomplish that which I please, and it shall prosper in the thing whereto I sent it. For ye shall go out with joy, and be led forth with peace: the mountains and the hills shall break forth before you into singing, and all the trees*

> *of the field shall clap their hands. Instead of the thorn shall come up the fir tree, and instead of the brier shall come up the myrtle tree: and it shall be to the* L<small>ORD</small> *for a name, for an everlasting sign that shall not be cut off."*
>
> Isaiah 55:8-13 (KJV)

No, my thoughts were not His thoughts because I didn't know the future—He did. He had plans, but I couldn't always see them clearly ahead of time. He described the mountains, the snow, and the fir trees in the Scripture He gave me. The last verse (verse 13) spoke to me of the Bible College—a work that would be "for a name, for an everlasting sign that shall not be cut off." God's Word taught to young men and women would go out to this generation and the next; it would go all around the world.

Don had loved our time in Capernwray, England, and had seen the value of Bible college because of its influence on his life. He had a vision and a desire to start one and see God do the same thing in the lives of others. The Lake Arrowhead Conference Center was a perfect place to begin this new venture.

Our nephew, David, came to the school and God did a lovely personal miracle for him. He had injured his hand one day and when others prayed for him, the Lord healed his hand. This greatly impacted his faith. After his time there, he and his wife Cindy went to France as missionaries during the early years of their marriage. Changed forever—we all were.

"The mountains are a good place to raise boys," my friend Laurel said. One would think all that fresh air and being outdoors would have been a haven of sorts. For us it was filled with adventures and excitement. Raising boys was never boring—quite the opposite. When Marcus was five years old he was in a bad accident falling off his bike headfirst going down a hill. Michael fell off a wall and fractured his skull at age three. And Donny was born with club feet, which took us on an adventure I will tell you about next.

But God! He kept a watch over them. I learned about the great love of God through my children. Even when they are naughty, we love them; we want the best for them. We sacrifice for them, but we must discipline them and teach them. God does this for His children and sets the example for us as parents. I love how Max Lucado says it: "God loves you just the way you are, but He *refuses* to leave you that way. He wants you to be just like Jesus."

Donny's Club Feet

Don said every time we moved, we picked up a new baby. So with our move to Lake Arrowhead came our third son. One evening near the end of my pregnancy, we were having dinner in San Bernardino and I was feeling more uncomfortable than usual. We decided to stop by the hospital for a quick check before the long drive home. It was a good thing we did! They encouraged me to stay that night, and at four o'clock in the morning Donny came into our lives. We were overjoyed!

A few hours later, our new pediatrician came to see me and asked if I had seen my baby's feet. I hadn't noticed anything unusual, and with him all swaddled up, I really didn't see much of his feet. He said, "Your baby has severe club feet and needs to see an orthopedic surgeon today." He seemed very concerned and urgent.

Well, I was exhausted and thought my baby was also after the ordeal of his birth. I asked if we could wait a couple days and go see our friend who was an orthopedic specialist. The doctor agreed to allow us to wait to see our friend, as long as we didn't wait too long. So when Donny was just five days old, Don and I took him to see Dr. Jack Pasqual in Westminster, California. Dr. Pasqual was an old friend of my dad's who had done his residency with him in Rochester, Minnesota. He was the one whom my dad told he wanted to move to California. He was also a Christian and went to Calvary Chapel.

At our initial consultation, he told us that he had only seen one other case that was as bad as Donny's. His feet were turned around backwards and faced each other like praying hands. The treatment to correct this would require a series of casts to gradually unscrew his feet and train them into the proper position. It would be a challenging and sometimes painful path, but would be the only way to keep him from spending his entire life crippled. Dr. Pasqual put us on a plan to come see him once a week so he could turn Donny's feet slightly and reset them in casts; eventually he would put him in bars and shoes. It would take a full year to correct his feet. So, for an entire year, I loaded the baby in the car, and we drove the two-hour drive down the mountain from Lake

Arrowhead. We would spend the night with my folks, go see the doctor the next morning, and then drive back home. Donny was so resilient; he was able to learn to scoot and crawl and never acted like there was anything abnormal.

A couple years after this ordeal, I saw a man at the Conference Center in Lake Arrowhead who had the same foot condition as my son at birth. He was in a wheelchair and would never be able to walk. I asked him about his condition and why they hadn't straightened his feet when he was a baby. He told me that he had grown up in Germany at a time when doctors there didn't know how to fix his feet. You see, baby's feet are pliable and moldable when they are little, but their bones stiffen as they grow. If this condition is not corrected at a very young age, it is not able to be reversed.

We are very grateful for the provision of God to have Donny's condition fixed, but there were times that were almost more than we could bear during that year of treatment. Sometimes the cast would pinch Donny's feet and cause him pain to the point of tears. One time I will never forget was very bad—he cried on and off for 24 hours straight. I called Dr. Pasqual and said, "Donny can't take this—none of us can take this anymore! Can I please bring him back in to see you? The casts are pinching him and causing him too much pain."

"I will tell you what," our compassionate doctor said. "I want you to take his casts off." He had taught me how to soak the casts in water to take them off. "Let's give him the week off.

You can bring him back next week for your normal appointment. We're going to give him a break." And what a break and relief that was for me!

Not long after that I was standing over Donny's crib on a beautiful, sunshiny day in Lake Arrowhead. I felt the Lord's presence in that room. He spoke to me in that still, small voice and said, "Do you see your baby's feet?"

"Yes, Lord, they are really bad."

And He said, "That is the way you were when you were born again. You came to Me crippled, born in sin, and I am going to spend your lifetime straightening your feet. Sometimes in your life you will cry out to Me and say, 'Lord, this lesson is too painful for me. I can't take it.' And I will take the casts off for a while and give you a break. But I will have to come back and finish teaching you those lessons so you can run with me on the high places." It reminded me of the verse in 2 Samuel that says: "He makes my feet like the feet of deer, and sets me on my high places. You enlarged my path under me; so my feet did not slip" (2 Samuel 22:34, 37). Have you ever seen a deer run in the mountains? They are so fast and agile and surefooted. The Lord wants to do the same beautiful thing with our lives; He wants us to learn to run with Him.

Not only did God provide for us in this trial, He used it to teach us great things, and He also prepared our hearts beforehand with comfort as well. Before this journey began, there was a man in our church named Bob Limley who had a vision about our son. He and his wife were expecting a baby about the same time. After the birth of both of our children, he came to me and told me the Lord had given him a vision. The Lord showed him that something was wrong with our baby when he was born, but He also told him there was no reason to worry; it would all turn out well. He saw a picture in the vision of Donny playing football. By God's grace, Donny's feet healed perfectly in the end, and all through high school he played football and loved it; it was his passion.

Michael's Salvation

Through it all, our time in Lake Arrowhead was a special and fruitful season in our lives. One very memorable Sunday stands out in my mind's eye. Don had already left for church; he always went early to go over his message and have some quiet time before the service. My unspoken job was to get the children ready and get them to church on time—which can be quite a feat with three little boys! Donny was a baby at the time and had his own room. Marcus and Michael shared a room down the hall.

After I had gotten Donny ready, I walked by the boys' room to see if they were dressed. I found them sitting on the floor talking intently—still in their jammies and nowhere close to being ready for church. Normally, I would have raised my voice and said, "Why aren't you guys getting dressed for church?! We are going to be late. Hurry up!" But wonderfully, God closed my mouth that day and I just stood there and listened. I was drawn in by the intensity of their conversation. I still remember the sound of Michael's voice. Sweet little Michael, at three years old, had an underdeveloped speech pattern where he couldn't pronounce his R's, so when he talked it sounded like he had a Boston accent.

As I listened, I heard him say to Marcus, "Mawky, I so sick in maw hawt."

"Michael, your problem is that you need to be born again."

Marcus encouraged him and gave him reasons why he needed to receive Jesus as his Lord and Savior. He was our little evangelist, even at a young age, and was completely unafraid of leading others to Christ. He knew it was truth and thought everyone else should know it too. It thrilled my heart to watch him using this evangelistic gift that God had given him as he shared with Michael.

Michael replied, "I know, Mawky, 'cause I so sick in maw hawt."

"I'm telling you, Michael, if you would just ask Jesus into your heart, you would feel so much better."

By this time, I had decided to join the group. I quietly sat down on their floor with them. At the next break in the conversation, I asked Michael, "Would you like us to pray with you to ask Jesus into your heart? Marcus and I will pray with you and you can do it right this minute. Do you want to pray?"

"Ah-huh, Mama, 'cause I so sick in maw hawt." So we bowed our heads and prayed the sinner's prayer.

As soon as we finished praying, we all looked up expectantly, only to see Michael vomit all over the floor. Ahhh! Needless to say, we missed church that morning. I guess his heart wasn't as sick as his stomach—Michael had the stomach flu!

But the treasure of that day was that Michael chose to become a child of God and has walked with the Lord ever since, and that Marcus' evangelistic heart brought him there. I love the evangelistic gift that God has given Marcus. He may have been a rascal to raise, but he sure knew how to love others to Jesus.

The End of Our Season in Lake Arrowhead

We lived in Lake Arrowhead for four years pastoring the church and building the Bible College, sometimes running the Conference Center. In 1979, the Lord placed a new burden and call on Don's heart for a small group of people in the valley of Redlands, California.

Our last Sunday at Lake Arrowhead, Don was preaching, and I was sitting in the half-round auditorium packed with 500 people; the crowd was so large, they were even sitting in the aisles. From where I sat, I could see most of their faces. I had grown to love them. As I scanned the room, I thought about each of them individually and all God had done in their lives. I knew their stories, where they had come from. Some worked at the post office. One family owned the grocery store. Another was a widower; I watched our church bring him meals and help him through his loss.

Another fellow was Don the barber. He served beer, played wild music, and had naked ladies on his drapes in his barbershop where he cut hair. He had started coming to our church because his girlfriend brought him. One Sunday he came up to Don and handed him his card. He said, "Let me give you a free haircut. I can't stand looking at you on Sunday mornings anymore with that hair" (which I had been cutting for him). Don went to see him and got a haircut—and Don the barber got saved and married his girlfriend. These dear people were our sheep, and they were precious to us.

On that last Sunday morning, as I looked into their faces, I remembered how I hadn't wanted to leave Calvary Chapel of Costa Mesa and our parents to come there. It brought me to tears as I thanked the Lord for allowing us to have this time here in Lake Arrowhead. "Lord, what if I hadn't come? I would not have gotten to know them and seen what You've done in their lives. What if I hadn't come?"

The Lord answered, "If you would not have come, I would have sent someone else and you would have missed all this." I would have missed the joys of knowing His people and seeing His handiwork.

Oh, Lord, please don't ever let me miss what You have for me. For Your ways are not my ways, nor my thoughts Your thoughts— they are so much greater!

12

Redlands, California

I will open rivers in desolate heights,
and fountains in the midst of the valleys;
I will make the wilderness a pool of water,
and the dry land springs of water.
Isaiah 41:18

The Lord called Don—and really all of our family—to Redlands. A small group of people were meeting together for a Bible study, and they had been praying that Don would come to start a church. They had been driving up to our church in Lake Arrowhead for some time. When they asked him to come, he quickly said, "Yes, I'm coming." The Lord had already prepared his heart and given us Scripture to confirm it. The verse He gave me was Isaiah 41:18: "I will open rivers in desolate heights, and fountains in the midst of the valleys; I will make the wilderness a pool of water, and the dry land springs of water." Once again, He described to me where we were going. Redlands is in a valley that can be very hot and dry.

As we left Lake Arrowhead to go to Redlands, the rest of the passage in Isaiah 41 had great meaning to us as well. It says, "That they may see and know, and consider and understand together, that the hand of the LORD has done this" (verse 20). We knew the Lord's hand was in this move and in the church He had called us to start; He had done this.

He graciously gave me another promise to hold on to in Isaiah 41:13: "For I, the LORD your God, will hold your right hand, saying to you, 'Fear not, I will help you.'" How often in life I have needed that verse.

On our first Sunday there were about 130 people who came to worship with us and study the Bible. We started out meeting at the University of Redlands in a classroom, and we eventually moved into the auditorium. Over the course of time, the church grew, and this led to needing a bigger building. God provided for us to buy the old Sunkist packing house, which later was used for the church and a school. *Calvary Chapel Magazine* wrote an article about our church and titled it, "Bearing Fruit for Jesus."

Shortly after we came to Redlands, we found a house for our family, and Don was ready to move that same week. For me, the timing couldn't have been worse. I wasn't ready or able to move; I had just come out of surgery to remove a kidney stone, which was an excruciatingly painful and draining ordeal. I had lost some blood and was completely exhausted—physically and emotionally. Sleep had eluded me for days. And to make matters worse, we had an energetic and precocious three-year-old (Donny), and a new puppy (Darcy). I was at my wit's end.

The new house didn't have a fence for the dog or Donny—who were both always running away. Moving again, and at this hard time, was more than I thought I could handle; it was overwhelming for me to even wrap my mind around it as I lay in bed, desperate for rest. Too exhausted to even formulate my thoughts clearly, I told the Lord, "I need help! First, I need sleep badly (I was wide awake in bed until 2 a.m.). I also need help with the dog, and I need help with Donny."

The next thing I knew, I awoke to the warm afternoon sun shining into my bedroom—I had miraculously slept all afternoon—and there beside my bed stood the dog trainer's wife. She told me that she and her husband wanted to take Darcy for the weekend. *Thank You, Lord!*

As soon as our rambunctious dog was out the door, the phone rang. On the other end of the line was a sweet friend who loved Donny and watched him for me at times. "I just talked to someone who saw you at the bank. She told me you looked awful. Can my husband and I take Donny for you for the weekend? How else can I help you?"

"Potty train him!" I said. "I'm too tired to deal with it."

She did.

Wow, Lord. All three prayers answered just like that, while I slept.

He knows what we have need of, and while we are yet speaking He answers. "It shall come to pass that before they call, I will answer; and while they are still speaking, I will hear" (Isaiah 65:24).

A Covenant of Peace

When my children were smaller, before high school and driver's licenses, I worried that they would always follow the Lord. One day, the Lord brought me to this verse in Isaiah that says, "All your children shall be taught by the LORD, and great shall be the peace of your children" (Isaiah 54:13). It brought me great comfort. I wrote their names beside that verse in my Bible, and I claimed it as my own. I knew God had given it to me to give me peace. As they grew, I watched the hand of the Lord work in my children's lives—sometimes for comfort, and sometimes for discipline.

Many years later, I realized that I still worried about them as adults even when they were on their own. I asked the Lord once again, "Are they going to be okay? Are all the boys always going to know You and walk with You?" The Lord really spoke to me. He said, "I already told you when I gave you Isaiah 54:13 when they were little."

I knew that passage by heart because it had become a promise I held on to, but I opened my Bible and read it again. Suddenly my eyes went back up to verse 10. It said, "'For the mountains shall depart and the hills be removed, but My kindness shall not depart from you, nor shall My covenant of peace be removed,' says the LORD, who has mercy on you."

What a confirmation from the Lord that His covenant of peace would not be removed because He had mercy on us as parents! His peace washed over my soul. I knew they would be okay, and chose to trust God at His Word.

Our oldest son struggled with us the most. He had to prove things for himself. At the end of his teenage years we sent him to camp in Northern California; that was where the Lord turned his life upside-down. He came home and decided to go to the School of Evangelism with Mike MacIntosh in San Diego, and from there he went into ministry for several years. "I think God wants me to minister to young people," he said when he returned from camp that summer. How awesome that God keeps our children in His sights! He hears our prayers.

Many years later, I was on the treadmill in Philadelphia during our pilgrim years, and I turned on the television to the 700 Club. Pat Robertson had a young man on the show sharing his testimony. His name was Mark Mohr. He had rebelled against his parents and Christianity all through high school. He said his parents sent him to a camp in Northern California in the last summer of high school, and he had made a best friend—Marcus.

I almost flew off the treadmill in shock because our son was named Marcus, and he had gone to that camp about that same time. At the camp, he had sat Marcus down and told him, "You and I are a lot alike." My eyes were glued to the TV. "But there is something different about you, and I can't put my finger on it.

THE TRUNK

What is it?" Marcus told him, "It's Jesus! That's the difference in me." Mark shared how Marcus had led him in the sinner's prayer. He never preached at him, he just loved him and answered his most important questions.

This young man went on to have a successful music band called Christafari (Christian reggae) that traveled all over the world. Over the course of his career, he has led thousands of young people to Christ. The Lord restored the years the locust had eaten in Marcus' life (see Joel 2:25). Even though he struggled in his high school years, God kept His hand on him and used him through it all. It's wonderful to see the hand of God moving in your children's lives.

Just think, when we introduce someone to Jesus, and they pray the sinner's prayer and ask Jesus to forgive their sins and come into their heart to be their Lord and Savior ... we don't know how many others they will lead to Christ.

One day a man came to see my husband. He said, "I was in your sixth grade Sunday school class years ago, and you prayed with me to receive Jesus that year. I just wanted you to know that you are a spiritual grandfather now. I grew up and went to seminary, and I am a pastor now. Don had felt like a failure as a Sunday school teacher that year; he was a brand-new Christian himself at the time. We never know where God will use us. Don didn't remember leading this man to Christ, but God did. The one you pray with to receive Jesus may become a minister, a missionary, a youth pastor, or the next Billy Graham—we never know.

13

Serpents and Poison

*And these signs shall follow them that believe;
in my name shall they cast out devils; they shall speak
with new tongues; they shall take up serpents;
and if they drink any deadly thing, it shall not hurt them;
they shall lay hands on the sick, and they shall recover.*
Mark 16:17-18 (KJV)

Growing up in the time of the Jesus People Movement, we had heard of miracles happening just like in the Bible. They didn't seem to happen too often in my life; or maybe they were happening and I just needed to stop and notice what God was doing all around us all the time. In the book of Mark, he talks about supernatural protection from serpents and poison. I hadn't noticed that verse before. One day, when my children were little,

THE TRUNK

it struck me in a new way which confirmed that same miraculous power in the lives of my children.

We had just moved from Lake Arrowhead to Redlands. One hundred years ago, presidents and railroads went through this quaint little town. The outskirts were lined with orange groves, and full of lovely old homes. We moved into a new home on the edge of town in the foothills.

Marcus was nine years old and was on his way home from school. I was on my way home to meet him but had stopped for a few minutes at a friend's house. I called to check on him.

"Mom," Marcus said, "I just got home and there was a baby snake at the front door, so I got the glass cage to put him in. When I picked up the snake it hissed at me, so I dropped it in the box and closed the lid."

"Don't open that lid!" I said firmly and rushed home.

When I got home I went directly into Marcus' room. There in the glass aquarium—with the lid on—was a very angry baby rattlesnake. I was shocked. As I watched it continue to coil and strike the glass, I shuttered in disbelief that it had not struck my son. Really amazing! It was the meanest, angriest reptile I had ever seen (and as a mother of three boys, I have seen a lot!).

We waited for Don to come home and take care of this poisonous creature. I told Marcus to stay out of his room and just stay in the hall and wait. I was pretty scared.

SERPENTS AND POISON

When his dad came home, he somehow got it into our bathroom. He dropped it—without touching it—into the toilet.

"You know, snakes can swim," I said.

He said, "No, I think only certain ones can swim, like water moccasins."

Well, that snake could swim all right! He quickly flushed it down the toilet. I have to tell you, after that, I never went into that room at night without turning on the light.

I later learned that baby rattlesnake venom is more poisonous than even adult rattlesnakes; it is more concentrated. How God wonderfully protected our son!

Around this same time, we began to have an ant problem in our kitchen. When you live in a new housing tract in the country, the critters come out because their homes are disturbed (and really, they were there first), and now there are new food sources as well.

We had lots of pesky little black ants that loved to send out scouts to find crumbs in the kitchen. I went to the store and picked up some ant poison baits. Our youngest son, Donny, who was three at this time, could get into anything. So I chose ant "hotels" thinking they would keep the poison away from little fingers. This is a device where the ants go into a little box and eat the poison, but children can't get to the poison because it is enclosed. Still, just to be careful, I placed them high in the kitchen to keep them out of sight and out of reach (or so I thought).

THE TRUNK

I was giving Michael a bath when Marcus came to the door. "Mom," he said, "what do we do if Donny is sucking on the ant poison?"

"He's not!" I pleaded, incredulously. "He is!" Marcus said.

I raced to the kitchen. I had put the poison up high where he wouldn't see it or get to it. But he had pulled up a chair and gotten it and was sucking on it. His saliva was going in and out of the little hotel, and he loved the sweet flavor.

I immediately called the pediatrician who advised me to take him to the nearest pharmacy. Once there, they gave him Ipecac to drink. We took him to the bathroom and let the medicine do its work. Then I had to take him to have tests done to see if he still had the poison in his system.

Yep! Arsenic poisoning! Miraculously, the induced vomiting had diluted it enough to save his life.

Not long after these two very serious and frightening incidents I was reading my Bible and came to these verses in Mark 16:17-18:

> *And these signs shall follow them that believe;*
> *in My name shall they cast out devils;*
> *they shall speak with new tongues;*
> *they shall take up serpents;*
> *and if they drink any deadly thing,*
> *it shall not hurt them;*
> *they shall lay hands on the sick,*
> *and they shall recover* (KJV).

SERPENTS AND POISON

Thank You, Lord Jesus, for watching over my children when I can't!

How unbelievable it is to me that I saw that verse after these two incidents. Both the serpent and the poison mentioned in one verse described what had just happened, and it said, "it would by no means hurt them."

I love that God so clearly speaks to us; I am always so amazed. Such a comfort! His faithfulness and care takes away fear. I'm so thankful I took the time—even in the midst of the craziness of life—to read God's Word. He is always good to speak comfort and encouragement into my heart and life. We need to spend time in God's Word daily! It is imperative, but oh, so rewarding!

Often I have been reading my morning devotions and find that He answers the exact questions that I have been stewing over in the night. The trials, the circumstances, the relationships: those things that are important to me are important to Him. I am amazed that His Word is so specific in speaking to us.

The Bible says that God's Word is living, and truly the Holy Spirit makes it alive; that is why it speaks to us daily to give us answers. Jesus in His wisdom did not leave us alone. He graciously left us His Word to show us the way. He knew we would need help. He gave us the Holy Spirit to teach us and guide us in that way. How incredible God is that He left us the manual, and a tutor. He thought of everything.

14

The Adventures of Donny

When Jesus saw him lying there ...
He said to him, "Do you want to be made well?"
John 5:6

It seems like just yesterday that our youngest son was called Donny. Today he is Don II, and at six-foot-two, you can be called whatever you want—he chose Don. But on this day, he was eight years old, and I called him Donny. The life of the number three boy is bound to be interesting, and his was filled with more excitement than most. His older brothers loved him, and loved to tease him; to say they tortured him would be an understatement. More often than not, they talked him into some daring endeavor, and he willingly jumped at the opportunity to thrill them.

One Sunday afternoon as Don and I were resting in the house, having no idea of what was going on outside, the

THE TRUNK

neighborhood kids gathered in the alley and talked him into jumping ten trash cans on his bike. Soon there was a loud knock at our door. We opened the door to find a neighborhood kid standing there telling us that Donny needed to go to the hospital. He had jumped the trash cans once and the whole gang, including his brothers, rooted him on: "Do it again!" (He was the youngest in the group.) Feeling like "Evel Knievel," and loving the exhilaration, he did it again; only this time his rear tire bumped the last trash can and threw him off his bike mid-air.

Thankfully, it was only a few stitches in his chin that were needed.

There were so many of these incidents, between his wandering off and the daring events, that with all three boys I felt like I was raising the Little Rascals.

The worst day, however, was when he was only eight years old. It was a warm September day. I remember the day well because it was my dad's birthday. We were expecting them for dinner, so I went to the market to get groceries.

Don was working out at the gym across the street at the University of Redlands. Michael was mowing the lawn for a neighbor a few doors down the street. Donny was alone for a rare brief moment; it was his chance to do what his brothers had told him not to do. They had built a ramp from the top of the swing-set in the backyard. He got his skateboard and went straight to the top of the ramp. He perched there for a few seconds—there was a thrill in the unknown—and then off he went. All went well at first as he flew down the ramp at high speeds across the backyard. Donny made the sharp turn at the driveway and began heading down the side of the house to the street. Just then, I returned from the grocery store and was pulling into the driveway. I decided to pull up all the way to the end of the driveway by the back door so I could unload the groceries directly into the kitchen. At that exact moment, Donny came flying around the corner on his skateboard. He yelled at the top of his lungs, and I honked (which did no good!), and … I went right over him with my car. He was silent. Terrified, I thought I was on top of his chest or stomach, so I quickly backed up. Thankfully, I wasn't on his torso, but I had driven over his leg. He had been on his knees on the skateboard and had put one leg out to stop himself, and that is the leg I drove over. When I backed up, I actually drove over his leg a second time; it was the second time when all the damage was done. I couldn't even see him because he was under my bumper; it was terrifying. He began yelling, "Mother!! You just drove over me and it really hurts!!!"

"Oh, thank You, Jesus—he is alive!" was my cry. I was in shock and shaking so badly. I yelled for help, but no one was home. I rushed out of my car and scooped him up into my arms. His leg just dangled in his jeans. *Lord, thank You. Thank You, he's alive!*

"Mother," he said, "just get me to the hospital." The eight-year-old was taking charge of the situation because I was losing it. I knew I could get him to the emergency room before an ambulance could get here, so I decided to put him in the car and go. The whole way to the hospital he screamed out every few minutes as the nerves in his leg sent signals to his brain.

About half a block down, I saw Michael mowing our neighbor's lawn. I stopped and called out to him. When he came to the car window, I told him what had just happened and asked him to quickly get his dad and tell him to come to the hospital. Michael looked from Donny to me in complete shock. He stopped what he was doing and ran to the University of Redlands gym. Don was working out in a gym full of people. Michael opened the door and yelled, "Dad, Mom just drove over Donny! You better get to the hospital!!" A dead silence fell over the gym—nobody moved. Don dropped everything and headed straight for the hospital.

I carefully drove to the hospital, stopping at every stop sign, until Donny's pain made him feel like his leg was going to explode. He finally said, "Mom, why are you stopping? Just get me to the hospital—don't stop!" I parked in front of the emergency room, not caring where or how and gave Donny permission to yell his head off if he wanted as I went inside to get help. Not waiting in line or feeling the need to be polite, I said, "I have just driven over my son!" and then they heard him scream. Dropping everything, the nurses ran to my car and got him on to a gurney. They took him right in without waiting for paperwork to be filled out—they said it could wait.

As soon as they gave him some pain killers, we were sent to get X-rays. The X-ray technician was careful and kind. I was so upset that I couldn't stand still, so I paced the floor. I thought that if I had been older, the stress would have put me in heart failure; my chest felt like it had a thousand-pound weight on it.

Thankfully, Donny was calm on the medicines, but awake. The X-rays revealed a spiral break—like a spiral staircase—going up his femur, and the fibula had snapped at the bottom. Needless to say, his entire leg was a mess. Miraculously, it hadn't touched his growth plate (that was the good news).

As the films were being made, a new X-ray technician came in to take the next shift. He saw me pacing and not crying and said, "Well, you are not very upset for having just driven over your child!" I stopped dead in my tracks and stared at him. The thought flashed through my mind, *Does he think that I did this on purpose? Will my name be in the paper tomorrow: "Pastor's Wife Drives Over Son on Purpose!"* This was a nightmare. I felt like I was in a bad dream and just wanted to wake up and have it disappear.

The technician who had been X-raying Donny came to my rescue and said, "Leave her alone. Can't you see she is really upset?!" I breathed a huge sigh of relief.

By the time we were back upstairs, Don had arrived. He tried to calm me down, but it wasn't working. I went to call my dad and told him, "Don't come for dinner. I have just driven over Donny!" When I returned to the room where Donny was laying on the examining table, Don had put a sheet over his head and said, "Shh." I looked at Don, and then at Donny; his tummy was shaking because he was laughing so hard (the pain-killers had kicked in). Don was trying to calm me down by getting me to laugh. I wasn't laughing. I was a wreck! "You're sick, Don!"—was all I could say; this humor wasn't working for me.

Shortly after, the doctor showed up in a foul mood; he had been forced to leave a dinner party with friends because of us. He jerked the X-rays off the chart to look at them. Then he threw his instruments around on the medical tray. He was so mad. Every crazy detail felt surreal to me. He put a cast on Donny that started at his toes and went all the way up his leg. When we finally arrived back home, we found a dear friend in the church cooking dinner for Marcus and Michael. *Thank You, Lord, for kindness from others.* We would have to celebrate my dad's birthday another day.

The next couple of days were very difficult with Donny in constant pain. He lived on the sofa downstairs in the family room and wouldn't tolerate being moved. The only time he let me move him was when a pretty strong earthquake hit, and we brought him outside until it was over. Almost every hour he would have the most horrific pain shoot through his leg. Two friends, who were medical professionals, came over to help me with him. They told me to leave the room when the sharp pain hit. I was feeling guilty, and it almost tore my heart out to hear him cry. Donny would ask me, "Mom, why did you drive over me?" I would explain this was a bad accident, and he had a run-in with my little Toyota pick-up and lost. What could I say?

That week was my turn to teach the ladies' Bible study at church—of course; it always seems that I teach on the worst weeks of my life. I told the ladies what had happened and asked them to pray that Donny's pain would stop. We needed a miracle! I had asked the doctor for stronger pain medicine, but he said Donny was on the strongest ones they could prescribe for him. He explained to me that this boy didn't just have a broken leg (in several places), but that his muscles had been smashed, and as they healed they were going into spasms (like Charley horses). There was no way to rub the muscles to ease the pain and cramping because of the large cast. The muscle pain and spasms were going to come and go for some time, at least a week, the doctor had said. He compared them to labor pains. So, with no solution or help for his pain, I desperately asked the ladies to pray for God to touch him.

Early the next morning as it was just getting light outside, I was up fixing breakfast. Donny was on the sofa in the next room. He called out to me, "Mom?"

"Yes, Donny?"

"I had this big hand on me last night, and it covered my whole body—it was God's hand; it was the warmest sensation I have ever felt."

I quickly came over to him and asked him to tell me what he had just said, barely believing what I thought I heard. He had my full attention.

"It was God's hand, Mom. He spoke to me and said, 'Do you want to be made well?'"

"I said, 'Yes, Lord, I do!' Mom, I have no more pain! It's gone." The pain never came back during the next ten weeks as he wore that cast and his bones and muscles were knit back together.

God knows how much we can take, and the pain had been pretty hard to handle. But more than that, this little boy felt the great big, healing hand of God at eight years old. It impacted his life in such a way that he grew up to never doubt Him. God showed Himself real and reached into our lives when we needed Him most. He reached into the lives of our children too.

Poor Gus

Two weeks later, I killed the cat in the dryer—by accident, of course!

It was a cool evening when I was quickly finishing up some laundry. Apparently the cat saw the open dryer door and jumped inside (maybe he thought it would be a warm place to rest). I never saw him. I walked by, shut the dryer door, and turned it on. Later that night, I came back to finish the laundry. When I went to get the clothes out of the dryer, there was an awful smell—like fish gone bad. As I pulled out my pink blouse, I saw a tiny spots of blood. *Hmm, what is that?* I wondered. I dug a little deeper into the dryer, and there was Gus (the cat) dead in the bottom of the machine. I was seriously scaring myself. *What is wrong with me? How could this be happening?* I walked into the family room where Donny was lying on the sofa. He was the only one home at the time. The other two boys were with their dad taking a sofa to someone. I told Donny, "I have just killed Gus!"

"Mom," the eight-year-old said, "you are freaking me out!"

"I am freaking myself out!"

I was too scared to tell the neighbors for fear I would be locked up for losing my mind. So I sat there and prayed and waited for Don and the boys to come home.

Don was so patient with me. He has a wonderful sense of humor which helped ease the tension a bit. He had already told the whole church I had driven over Donny. He told them he had sat me down and said, "Jean, disciplining these boys is one thing, but driving over them has got to stop." Don even had a T-shirt made for Donny that had a cartoon picture of him on crutches with a large cast on his leg. At the top of the shirt it read, "My mother did it." Now, two weeks later, he announced that I had killed the cat in the dryer that week. How would you like this woman to be your pastor's wife? I sure didn't have much credibility left.

Once, while we were in the waiting room at the doctor's office, a boy about his age was sitting next to him with a cast on his arm. "What happened to you?" Donny asked.

"Soccer," the boy replied. Then, seeing Donny's huge cast, the dreaded, inevitable question came, "What happened to you?"

"Oh," Donny replied, "My mother drove over me."

The expression on his mother's face was priceless. She had been looking ahead casually listening to the boys when that sentence hit. She stared straight ahead in shock and then slowly turned her head to stare at me. She never did say a word, but neither did I—awkward silence at the shock of it all.

During the long season of recovery, Donny learned to sit and play with Legos for eight hours a day. My mother-in-law thought it was a good thing for a very active, hyper child to learn to sit still and be creative. He lived on the sofa for weeks; he celebrated his ninth birthday there. He wore the cast from his toes to his hip for ten full weeks until his leg was mended.

Donny learned firsthand how big His God is and that He is alive and real. He learned that God could heal from pain. There are hardships and struggles and pain in this world, but God can work them for good if we trust Him. He said, "All things work together for good to those who love God" (Romans 8:28). That verse implies things aren't always good, but God doesn't waste our struggles and trials. He uses them so often to teach us things, if only we will listen. And the storms strengthen our roots and develop character. When we allow our roots to grow deep down into Him and His Word, we won't snap and break when the fierce winds blow.

Needless to say, I was very much on edge and emotionally frazzled after driving over Donny and killing Gus. Frankly, I was worried about myself. *What was wrong with me?* I thought. So I was a bit nervous, okay, a lot nervous for a while.

A Dead Rat

As I pull this part of my story out of my trunk, I am ashamed and humbled—but God, I have found, teaches us in our failures, and while I would not consider this a treasure, looking back it really was. I believe that when God speaks to us in our failures, He is giving us a gift to teach us to be more like Him and less like ourselves.

Being so anxious, I thought if someone popped a balloon next to me I would jump fifty feet in the air, and that is pretty much what happened. Our family room was filled with balloons from the loving church people who had sent "get well" wishes to Donny. One night after dinner, a couple of weeks after Donny's accident, I was cleaning up the dishes when Michael (who was eleven at the time) accidentally popped a balloon in the living room. I practically jumped out of my skin; it felt like someone had shot me. I rushed into the living room and got mad at Michael. Don came into the room when he heard me and said, "Michael, I don't know what you have done, but you have really upset your mom. You better go to your room." All the boys in my house fled; that is what boys do when women lose it.

After giving myself a little time to calm down, I went upstairs to check on Michael. We sat on his bed and talked for a good while. His heart was so sad. He had been crying and probably wondering what in the world he had done wrong. As we talked, he unloaded about the tough things he had been going through at school, and my heart broke. Michael was the sweetest, most sensitive little boy. He has loved the Lord for as long as I can remember. My mom used to say, "Michael is so good, it hurts." We were all feeling the weight of this painful trial. How could

THE TRUNK

I take out my stress on this sweet child? I wanted to cry myself. I apologized and just sat there and listened to him talk. Chuck Swindoll gave a message on raising children once that I haven't forgotten. He said it is so important to sit on your kid's bed at night before they go to sleep and just be quiet and listen. They don't want to go to sleep anyway, so they will talk. And if you don't interrupt and pass judgment, you will learn a lot about your child.

When I went to bed that night, the Lord began to speak to me about my reaction to the balloon incident that day. He reminded me of something that had happened the summer before. One day I noticed a terrible odor in the house, so I went in search of the source in the boys' bedrooms. There, in the wastepaper basket, was a dead rat! He had been there for a few days. The warm summer weather didn't help. It gets pretty hot in Redlands, and we lived in an old house with the kids' bedrooms upstairs. Marcus had some pet rats in a cage and apparently one had died. The boys had simply thrown the rat in their trash basket to dispose of it. I carefully transferred it into a dust pan and started to carry it down to the garbage. As I headed down the stairs, I accidentally tripped, and the rat fell on to the stairs. I watched in horror as maggots scurried into the carpet. This was a job for someone with a stronger stomach than me! Needless to say, I called the boys and had them finish the job with instructions to never leave dead things in their room again—they need to go all the way outside into the garbage cans.

As I was lying in bed that night, the Lord reminded me of that awful experience. He said, "Remember how bad that dead rat smelled?"

"Oh yes, Lord, it was really terrible."

"That," He said, "is how your attitude smelled in the house tonight to your children."

I am a visual learner, and the picture painted for me was very clear. The damage we can do to those we love when we get angry leaves a bad smell that can linger for years to come. I don't want to be remembered as an angry woman. I want to end up a sweet, old lady like my precious mother-in-law.

I am so thankful for God's correction. "Behold, happy is the man (or woman) whom God corrects; therefore do not despise the chastening of the Almighty" (Job 5:17). God's corrections can also be our treasures. Welcome them.

15

San Jose, California

*Those from among you shall build the old waste places;
you shall raise up the foundations of many generations;
and you shall be called the Repairer of the Breach,
the Restorer of Streets to Dwell In.*
Isaiah 58:12

Sometimes I think I am married to a man who is like the apostle Paul; he loves challenges and loves to start churches. He loved to start things like the Calvary Chapel Bible College (which is now in Murrieta, California), and like the churches in Lake Arrowhead, Redlands, and other places. If he did not go, he sent others. His heart was to see people taught the Word of God. The church in San Jose, California, however, was a stretch beyond what he had done thus far, beyond what we both had ever dreamed.

We had been pastoring the church in Redlands for eleven years. Don was getting restless. He had just returned from flying all over the nation seeing hungry churches and hurting people. His heart was grieved as he came back to his spiritual Disneyland, where wonderful churches were found on practically every corner, and he wanted to help. One afternoon while we were out in our backyard talking, he said, "I want to go someplace where there is a need." One year earlier he had said the same thing to me and I panicked. I thought, *I can't leave my mother* (she had Alzheimer's), *and Marcus wants to get married. I'm not ready. Michael and Donny are in high school and junior high—critical ages to be uprooted.* So he didn't bring it up again for a while.

I brought up some great reasons why we shouldn't do this again, only this time he said, "Why are you so negative?" I had no answer. I walked back into the house and heard the Lord speak clearly to my heart and say, "WHY *ARE* YOU SO NEGATIVE?"

When people say things, we argue. When God says something, we must listen.

I had to get this settled in my heart. I wanted to be obedient to the Lord. So I walked back outside and said, "Go ahead and talk to Chuck Smith and see what he says." I wasn't too worried because I thought, *Nothing could possibly happen for six months. I have plenty of time to adjust to the idea of moving again.*

Within the next couple of days he went to see Pastor Chuck. Don walked in and said, "Send me someplace no one else wants to go." Don said he would never forget the smile on Chuck's face as he said, "Have I got a place for you!"

SAN JOSE, CALIFORNIA

A minister had recently come to Chuck and offered him his church in San Jose, California. The church had been a part of the community for over eighty years; it was a large and beautiful church situated on ten acres of land in the heart of the Silicon Valley. The sanctuary sat about nineteen hundred people and was adorned with beautiful stained-glass windows. But it was also over $8 million in debt, and sadly, they were going to lose their building within the next few weeks. It cost nearly $56,000 a month just to keep the doors open, and that didn't include paying the staff salaries or even turning on the lights. Chuck told Don, "You can have it and turn it into a Calvary Chapel. We just have to put up a million dollars to save it from going back to the bank. We will loan you the money, but down the road you will have to pay it back."

Don wasn't very interested. He loved to start ministries, but not finish them. He didn't believe in putting new wine in old wineskins. He thought it was far easier to pull off a new birth than a resurrection. He also knew Chuck had offered it to another pastor (a friend of ours), Jon Courson. "Let Jon take it," Don said, and then drove home. On that quiet drive the Lord convicted him and spoke to his heart: *You asked Me where to go and now you don't want to listen.*

Okay, Lord, he thought. He called Chuck back and said, "If Courson doesn't take it, I'll look at it."

Jon went to visit the church to see if this was where the Lord was leading him. He had gotten saved at that very church in junior high school, and we thought he might be interested in becoming their new pastor. Jon called us after he had gone down to visit the church, and I happened to answer the call: "Well," Jon said, "I don't like money problems or three-piece suits (which they wore in that church). My wife and I think Don's a perfect fit for that church. We'll be praying for you!" I had to smile.

We went to visit the church with my dad and our two youngest boys. The people of this church desperately needed love and help; it was like they had been in a bad accident. Our hearts went out to them and wanted to see these precious sheep made whole. The church had five thousand members and had just built a new sanctuary, which was beautiful, but they had way overspent. On top of that, they had a church split which left them with only a few hundred people.

Within about three weeks, he was there full-time as their new pastor. Sometimes he slept at my brother and sister-in-law's home about forty-five minutes away, and sometimes he slept on the pews at the church until he found a house to rent. Once he found the house for our family, Don Jr. and I came to San Jose, along with our cat. We left Michael in Redlands with my dad to finish his junior year of high school. Marcus was married by this time and remained in Southern California.

Of all the churches Don started, and all the schools and ministry adventures, this one would teach me like no other. Little did we know how hard this would be, how long it would take, and how utterly dependent upon God we would become.

Looking back on our eleven years there, I would never trade them for the lessons I learned and the miracles of God's provision that I saw with my own eyes.

As I pull this testimony out of my old attic trunk, it is a great treasure, for it caused me to truly see the faithfulness of God. Sometimes the hardest experiences end up being our most valuable lessons!

Challenges awaited us that we couldn't have anticipated, but God walked with us each and every day. At its height, the church had been at an attendance of about five thousand people. And now, with the church split and terrible debt, there were only 388 people left, according to one usher; even some of those people left after we came. It was a difficult time. One member that came with the building told us over dinner, "You know, every day the doors are open to that building is a miracle." He was right. But we serve a God who is in the business of miracles! One Sunday, nineteen people left simply because we had closed off the balcony section. The large beautiful sanctuary with gold chandeliers and red carpeting weren't enough to keep the people there. They needed a shepherd to lovingly lead and teach them God's Word.

Don faithfully began to minister to the church; he didn't miss a Sunday for the first year, and we didn't take a salary for three years. During that time, God gave me a verse that described the church so well—"Those from among you shall build the old waste places; you shall raise up the foundations of many generations; and you shall be called the Repairer of the Breach, the Restorer of Streets to Dwell in" (Isaiah 58:12).

The church was eighty years old—the "old waste places." It had five office complexes throughout the property. Don took several of these and turned them into apartments for the staff to offset the fact that we couldn't pay them much. Here again the verse held true—the "Restorer of streets to dwell in."

Don held a Bachelor of Science degree from Cal Poly in business administration and now we knew why. He put his business mind in gear and went to work, saving in every area he could: putting the staff in the office complex in the building, not taking a salary, and not leaving town, using volunteers. But no matter how we scrimped, saved, and planned, without God it was impossible.

God was doing a work that would bring Him glory and give a foundation to the generations to come. We simply had to be obedient to the call He had placed on our hearts and the work He had placed in our hands. It wasn't an easy road, but it was so fulfilling and faith building to see Him bring beauty from ashes. I often thought of the story of Jesus and the five loaves and two fishes; with thousands of people to feed, it was easy for the disciples to wonder, "What is this amongst so many?" Yet, in God's hands, even our meager offering can bring about great things. I had to learn patience.

Today our son, Michael, pastors the church which is full of wonderful young families and has a great Christian school. We

SAN JOSE, CALIFORNIA

are so thankful we stepped out into those deep waters as God led us. Just like it says in Isaiah, "to give them beauty for ashes, the oil of joy for mourning, the garment of praise for the spirit of heaviness; that they may be called trees of righteousness, the planting of the Lord, that He may be glorified" (Isaiah 61:3, KJV).

16

God's Message Hasn't Changed

*Most assuredly, I say to you, unless a grain of wheat falls
into the ground and dies, it remains alone;
but if it dies, it produces much grain.
He who loves his life will lose it, and he who hates his life
in this world will keep it for eternal life.*
John 12:24-25

We had been in San Jose for about a year when God pierced my heart with a word of correction, a word of reminder of something I had stored in my trunk from high school. Our first Christmas in San Jose in our little rental was not what I had hoped for or expected. I hadn't felt like decorating at all. So some dear friends of ours, Gail and Steve Mays (the pastor of Calvary Chapel South Bay), came to visit and persuaded me to buy lights for the tree and decorate it—it was lovely. While they were there, I remember Steve sitting in our living room saying, "You are going to live in this house for three years." He said it with such conviction; I tucked it away in my heart. I didn't believe him—and really, I didn't want to believe him. The house was small, and there were beetles all over the garage floor—I was hoping they weren't cockroaches. This was not the living situation I had grown used to, and I was having a hard time accepting that fact.

It was a cold winter day as I headed into church that Sunday. And before I could even get through the door, a woman stopped me to tell me they were leaving the church. She was one of my new friends there. We had often gone bike riding together. *Not another one, Lord.* (She and her husband had come with the building. There were those who came with the previous church, "the building," and those who came after, the new ones.)

"Don't misunderstand," she sympathized. "We love your husband's teaching, but we don't care for the worship."

I was so discouraged. We had one more family leaving the church, and leaving us with this gigantic, beautiful building and its gigantic, awful debt! As I looked around the room and thought of my dear husband pouring out his life for this church, I got so upset. I thought, *These people incurred this debt, and then they looked at my husband and waved goodbye. They said, "It's your problem now!" and walked out the door—without a care in the world.* I quietly slipped out the door into the church office as I began to cry. I'm not a crier, but that day it was more than I could

GOD'S MESSAGE HASN'T CHANGED

bear. As I stood there trying to collect myself, in walked Loren, our precious young assistant pastor. He too had come with the building, but he stayed and was such a blessing to us.

"Are you okay?" he asked.

"Yes, I will be fine. But sometimes it just gets to me," I said through tears.

"Sometimes," he said, "it gets to all of us." *Well,* I thought, *at least we're not alone.*

After a moment of regaining my composure, I went back into the sanctuary and stayed through the sermon to support my husband. But then I slipped out during the closing prayer and went home. I did not want to talk to anyone else that day. I knew God was in charge, and I knew He was weeding through the flock and that some would leave. But it still hurt, and I was frustrated that it hurt so much.

I went straight home and put on my coziest sweats (which I like to call "legal pajamas") and sat in front of the fireplace. "Lord," I prayed, "just tell me one more time that You want us here!" I was so discouraged; I really needed to hear from Him.

Then He answered in that still, small voice that grips your heart.

Do you remember in high school when you were fifteen years old and you said that you would go into full-time Christian service? You said you would go anywhere I sent you. Yes, I remembered saying that to God.

THE TRUNK

Then the question came from God:

What happened to you? What has changed?

Silence. I remembered that night kneeling by my bunk bed in the dark at HDA giving Him my whole life—all control.

What has happened?! God said again.

"I got soft," I whispered. "I have become accustomed to two cars in the garage, a swimming pool, a nice house, and a salary from the church." I liked all the creature comforts that surrounded me. But He had called me to be a soldier in His army, and I had been enjoying the ride rather than training for the battle. And a soft sissy has no place in His army.

It reminded me of a devotional I had read: "I fear I am a soldier for the parade, not the battle. I love the bands, the flags, the cheering; but the gunfire makes me nervous!"[1]

I'm sorry, Lord. I'm so sorry. Forgive me. Help me to be strong.

Soon after that encounter with the Lord, someone from Southern California dropped off a package for us at the church. We never did find out who it was from, but I knew the Lord had sent it to lift our hearts, and He had used some godly saint as His instrument. In it was everything our family loved; nuts for Don, special sweets for the kids, and little things that made our day.

Tucked inside was a book for me titled, *Evidence Not Seen*, by Darlene Deibler Rose.[2] I love to read missionary stories, and

---

1 W. Glyn Evans, *Daily with the King* (Chicago: Moody Press, 1989), 79.
2 Darlene Deibler Rose, *Evidence Not Seen* (New York: HarperCollins, 2003), 148-151.

this book became a prized possession. It is the dramatic story of the first American woman to become a missionary in the Baliem Valley of New Guinea. She and her husband had just graduated from Bible college, gotten married, and begun serving the Lord together when war broke out and forced their separation and imprisonment. She was sent to one camp, and he was sent to another. Sadly, they never saw each other again. She survived for four years in horrific conditions in Japanese prison camps in the jungles of New Guinea; sometimes her only food was maggot-infested rice.

My trials in life were absolutely nothing compared with hers! The suffering she endured was unthinkable. But God saw her and kept her, and even in that horrible and cruel prison camp, He worked miracles—though she would remain there for four long years.

One story in particular challenged me and encouraged my own dwindling faith. She was literally starving to death and extremely malnourished in solitary confinement, and very ill. As she sat there alone, she watched through a window as another prisoner smuggled in a bunch of bananas through the fence in the complex. After seeing that, all she could think about was bananas, and in her hunger, she began to crave them. She asked the Lord to give her just one banana. Her daily food was one bowl of rice porridge, which was barely enough to keep her alive. As she prayed, she reasoned through how impossible the situation was and saw no way it could be done without a guard losing his life or being beaten because of her request. So she all but gave up the thought and prayer. Shortly after, a Japanese officer whom she had known at another camp came to visit her. When he left, her guard returned and placed a bundle on the floor of her cell. To her utter amazement, there before her was the largest pile of bananas she had ever seen; she carefully counted out ninety-two bananas! How extravagant is our God! She wept with gratitude and humility as she praised God for His ability to do the impossible, and for His great love for her. Those precious bananas sustained her until her release from that prison cell.

I finished that book and realized my life was luxurious compared to her suffering. *Forgive me, Lord. Make me a soldier in Your great army in these times. May I never doubt You or complain again in this Silicon Valley. This is Your church and Your ministry. Make me a good steward and a servant. Help me to press on in the joy of the Lord and do what You need me to do to help my husband and this ministry.*

It is in the dying to ourselves—our wants and selfish thoughts—that we live. It is in the giving up that we receive. It is in the dying that we live. Just as it says in John 12:24-25, "unless a grain of wheat falls into the ground and dies, it remains alone; but if it dies, it produces much grain. He who loves his life will lose it, and he who hates his life in this world will keep it for eternal life." Is this not what Jesus did? He gave up heaven to come to earth to find us.

Three years after coming to San Jose, our house in Southern California finally sold, and we found a wonderful house across from a creek. It was a repossession owned by the bank, and it was perfect. Just as Steve Mays had said—we would be in the rental for exactly three years; and it was exactly three years.

Our church grew as days turned into months, and months turned into years. We had large seminars for the men and women that filled the 1,900-seat sanctuary to the brim. Our women's ministry grew tremendously and was such a blessing. Don pastored that church for eleven years. They were some of the richest years in ministry as we witnessed the greatness and faithfulness of God—more treasures to pull out of my trunk to testify of what God has done. As challenging as it was at times, I wouldn't trade that season for anything—not for all the gold in the world.

17

"Never Get Better"

*I will bring the blind by a way they did not know;
I will lead them in paths they have not known.*
Isaiah 42:16a

When we first came to San Jose, one of the saints in the church said, "There is a cloud of darkness that hangs over the Bay Area. There isn't much spiritual life here." As I watched during our eleven years there, I noticed ministers didn't last long—on average just three years; health, moral issues, and many other reasons caused them to leave.

Don too had some serious health issues during our time there. I really thought the devil was trying to kill him. I remember thinking, *We aren't leaving until God tells us to!* I remembered Job saying, "Though He slay me, yet will I trust Him" (Job 13:15). That is the bottom line, isn't it? In the midst of the trials of life is the place where trust and faith begin.

THE TRUNK

Don was upstairs on the treadmill when he began to feel dizzy. He said to himself, *you slob. Keep going!* So he kept going despite the light-headedness. Afterwards he came downstairs to where I was in kitchen and his eye was bright, blood-red.

"What's wrong with your eye?" I asked.

"I don't know," he said. "I feel dizzy."

In the next 24 hours he began losing his vision in his right eye. We went to an ophthalmologist and found out he had suffered a stroke in his eye and it had hemorrhaged, causing him to lose most of the vision in that eye. After the doctor examined his eye, I began to ask him if he could do anything to bring his sight back. "What if we fed him carrots and healthy things? Would that help?" I was grasping at straws, desperately trying to fix him, and really unwilling to accept the diagnosis.

"No," the doctor said. "Nothing will help." As I kept asking questions, not wanting to hear what he was telling us, Don sat very quietly without saying a word. Later he told me that as I was arguing with the doctor, the Lord had shown him a door and over the top it said, "Never get better." He opened it and asked Don, "Will you step through the door?"

Don answered, "Lord, I will step through it if You will go with me." Then the Lord gave him peace and acceptance. In a moment one's life can change, can't it? Many times I have thought of those words "never get better." But the comfort is this: we do not have to go through those doors alone—He will go with us.

"NEVER GET BETTER"

It is amazing how your brain adjusts and compensates to losing vision in one eye. Today, Don can do everything he did before and often forgets his right eye doesn't see as well. But when it first happened, he lost his depth perception and often stumbled into furniture. I had to do the driving for a while; it took months for his brain to adjust and for him to feel like normal again, but it did come.

We took a trip to Southern California that summer to vacation with Don's sister and her husband (John and Marilyn) on a boat at Catalina Island. Mike and Sandy MacIntosh joined our families as well. While we were together, Mike had to slip away to do a beach baptism one night. He had been teaching a Bible study for college-aged kids at John and Marilyn's house for a few years, and that night was their baptism at Corona del Mar beach. Mike asked Don to go with him to the baptism, and Don agreed to go despite his inner-turmoil over it; to get to that beach you had to take a narrow, windy and rocky path down a cliff. For Don, who still struggled with his depth perception, and couldn't see the path very well in the dark, this was very difficult. Falling down in front of a bunch of college kids would be highly embarrassing!

"Jesus, help me." He whispered. At that moment, he said the most incredible thing happened; it was as if the Lord Jesus stood next to him and helped him down the path. He never tripped even once. The next morning in my quiet time I read the verse in Isaiah 42:16 that says, "I will bring the blind by a way they did not know; I will lead them in paths they have not known. I will make darkness light before them, and crooked places straight. These things I will do for them, and not forsake them." The Lord had certainly walked beside Don and helped him down that path that night.

I love how the Lord will never leave us or forsake us. He walks through doors with us of "never get better" and down paths we are unsure of. We are all blind to the future, but He will lead us there too—and all the way home. We need not fear, He is right here with us.

After losing the vision in his right eye, Don began to memorize Scripture—several psalms a week. He would tape them to the treadmill and memorize them as he exercised. One night I tested him to see how far he had gotten. He had memorized five psalms that week, and I asked him to quote them to me. As he recited them perfectly, I thought, *How does he do that? I struggle to learn one verse.* Those verses were going to be a great comfort to him (and others) as he would soon face another physical trial a year or two down the road with his lungs. The psalms always bring comfort, don't they?

18

Miracles in the Silicon Valley

> *Thus says the* L<small>ORD</small>, *your Redeemer,*
> *and He who formed you from the womb:*
> *"I am the* L<small>ORD</small>, *who makes all things,*
> *who stretches out the heavens all alone,*
> *who spreads abroad the earth by Myself.*
> Isaiah 44:24

When I was a little girl, San Jose was an old agricultural valley known for its almond groves and vineyards. Today, it is called the Silicon Valley because the sand—silicon—was discovered there. Southern California is known for its deserts, mountains, and beaches. But the Silicon Valley is known for its computer industry that draws technological minds from all over the world; it was the beginning of the communication highway. Semiconductor, Apple and other computer companies make their home there.

THE TRUNK

People come from all over the world to work there, and it has been reported to have the most PhDs of any city in the United States. It was here in this setting of the cutting edge, brilliant-minded computer industry that God was doing miracles in my small and simple world. He would faithfully—and oftentimes, miraculously—provide for us each step of the way.

In the first few years, I often answered phones in the church office simply to help and also to meet people. Those of the congregation that stayed were very sweet to us. Once when I was sick, I remember a steaming pot of delicious homemade chicken soup being dropped at my front door. Another time they lovingly cleaned our house. There were many special times of fellowship when they invited us to their homes for dinner. And as our lives became connected, we grew to love them.

One of the most amazing things about this season in our lives was watching God provide every day for us, the staff and the church as a whole. His provision was always so specific and perfect.

One unforgettable Monday morning we were short $10,000 on church bills—what seemed like an unsurmountable sum. An envelope arrived at the church that very morning with a check in it for exactly $10,000.

One day a pastor friend of ours from Arizona called Don and asked him about our church debt and all. After he heard the story he said, "You know, our church has a debt of $100,000 and I have been feeling terrible about it. After hearing your story, I feel great!" He laughed and hung up the phone. I'm so glad we could help our friend with a dose of perspective! I had to laugh.

There was a time when the boys needed clothes for their grandparents' fiftieth wedding anniversary party; it was a grand affair in Southern California at an elegant club, which required they be dressed appropriately. I went to Nordstrom Rack to find all the things the boys needed—shirts, slacks, coats, and shoes. I did the best I could under the circumstances, but it still cost about $400. When we arrived home, there was a check in the mail for the exact amount I had just spent.

Another time one of the boys needed their wisdom teeth pulled out. By faith we took him to the dentist and had the necessary work done on his teeth. And once again there came a check in the mail for the exact amount of the dentist bill. Amazing.

Our youngest son was taking close notice of God's perfect care for us, and storing it in his heart; these things shaped his character. He would comment, "Mom, isn't that exactly what we spent?" God's miraculous provision time and again left us speechless and thrilled our hearts. We never would have known it if we hadn't needed it so desperately! Even recounting these stories to you today is bolstering my faith. God never stops being all that we need; He is the All-Sufficient One. His past faithfulness in our lives is undeniable and unforgettable. We can trust Him no matter the situation, for the present as well as the future.

THE TRUNK

Years later, my daughter-in-law, Brenda, came over wearing a darling dress she had had her eye on at The Loft. With a price tag of $120, she quickly set it back down and walked away; it was more than she could afford. Not long after, she was shopping at the outlet, and there on the rack, to her utter amazement, was the same dress—in her exact size—for only a little over $20. My youngest son was listening to her tell me this story. He looked her in the face and without hesitation said, "That is what God does for you when you serve Him." He too had lived this journey with us for the last ten years—he got it.

We sometimes think life is hard, and we worry about our kids suffering in one way or another, but the truth is, watching God provide was the best lesson in the world for all of us. Our faith grew and our trust in God developed depth. Each of our boys would take these lessons with them into their own families one day.

I have learned the profound truth that God never just moves the husband, but He moves the whole family. He has a place for each member of the family and meets the needs of each person individually. He didn't just call Don, but He called all of us and had good plans and purposes in mind. In Jeremiah 29:11, we read, "For I know the thoughts that I think toward you, says the Lord, thoughts of peace and not of evil, to give you a future and a hope." He has a future and a hope for each of us. God used Marcus to lead the youth group for a time. And He brought Michael's precious wife, Brenda, into his life.

My faith wasn't always strong during this time, but just when I needed to see His hand in our lives, He would blow my mind again with His loving provisions.

On a busy weekday, I ran out to get some groceries—company was coming the next day for dinner. As soon as I made it out to the parking lot and got into my car, I remembered that I had forgotten to buy tomatoes and cucumbers for the salad. I was too weary and rushed to go back into the store, and the stress of spending more money stopped me in my tracks—I just sat there. Then I prayed, "Lord, You know I'd like tomatoes and cucumbers. If it's Your will, would You please provide them?" I remember sitting there smiling, thinking, *I wonder how God is going to do this one.* I had seen so many miracles, and He had been so faithful; I knew that He wanted to bless His children and would lovingly take care of even this little thing that was important to me. Then I drove home and went on with my day.

That evening I went to church for our midweek Bible study. After the service ended a sweet Chinese lady came over and handed me a brown paper lunch bag. "What's this?" I asked.

In broken English she said, "Oh, it's nothing—just a little something from my garden." To my great delight, I peeked inside the bag and saw beautiful, large, home-grown tomatoes and cucumbers. The cucumbers were even the special hothouse type (burp-less). I remember feeling humbly amazed as tears filled my eyes. I told this precious sister, "You will never know what this means to me. Thank you so much!"

Another time a missionary called our church and talked with one of the assistant pastors. He had heard that we had a food bank and a ministry of giving things to those in need. He asked if we had a wheelchair that we could donate to someone in great need. Our assistant pastor knew we didn't have one at the time, but told him we would call him if we ever got one.

That very same week a wheelchair was left in front of our food bank offices—we had never had anything like that donated before; it was usually just food and clothing. The Lord had provided a wheelchair. Our assistant pastor called the missionary to tell him we had a wheelchair, but the foot pedals were missing. His enthusiastic reply was, "That's perfect! The person on the mission field who needs it doesn't have any feet!" Oh, the providence of our God—such details He puts together! I suppose it is easy for the One who created everything to lead, guide, and provide and put such awesome plans together so perfectly. But it is beyond breathtaking for me to have watched and seen it with my own eyes time and time again. I will never trade those years for anything.

Michael, our middle son, was graduating from high school during our second year in San Jose. We had always promised him we would send him to college, but we were in a place financially where we couldn't afford it. We hadn't sold our home in Southern California since we moved to San Jose; it was a bad housing market. And we also hadn't taken a salary yet as we worked to help get the church out of debt and back on track.

One day, I went to the Lord about this and asked if He could make a way for Michael go to college. He had been accepted at Vanguard University in Costa Mesa, California. But how could we afford the tuition at a private school?

Graduation time rolled around faster than seemed possible. I remember sitting at the baccalaureate ceremony listening to the speakers and thinking about Michael's future. At the end of the ceremony, they began announcing college scholarships that were being given to some of the students. There were ones for $500, maybe a $1,000, but not much money for college, I thought. We had not applied for scholarships; I didn't even know they had them at the time. Then, toward the end of the list, they announced $9,500 was going to Michael McClure. I couldn't believe it! Between his cross-country scholarship and this money, his first year of college was completely covered. Again tears came as I thought about my little conversation with God asking Him to provide for Michael's desire to attend college. I couldn't believe I had heard correctly. Then Jesus spoke to my heart and said, "What you don't know is that I love Michael more than you do."

Oh, thank You, Lord—You love our kids! You love them more than we could ever love them. Your love will take care of them all of their lives.

19

A Refuge in All Our Ways

*Because you have made the LORD, who is my refuge, even
the Most High, your dwelling place,
no evil shall befall you,
nor shall any plague come near your dwelling;
for He shall give His angels charge over you,
to keep you in all your ways.*
Psalm 91:9-11

When we first started out on this journey to walk with the Lord and go wherever He called us, we didn't expect or plan on the path He would choose. Isn't that how it often happens? But as we have walked by faith, God has led us faithfully and provided for our needs, and specifically for our dwelling places. We need not fear or worry when we place our lives in His loving hands.

Don had pastored the church in San Jose for about ten years, and our boys were all grown up and out of the house. Don

THE TRUNK

had talked on and off about moving closer to the church, and downsizing. One Sunday afternoon when Michael and Brenda were over for brunch, there was a knock on the front door. It was a real estate agent who had clients with her who were interested in buying a house in our neighborhood. Surprisingly, they asked if they could look at our house. We had never listed it or told anyone that we might sell it. How interesting! Don willingly showed them the house while the rest of us quickly cleaned up the kitchen.

The sweet, young couple really liked our house. They had been looking for a place with a bedroom and bathroom on the first floor (which we had) because their elderly mother was moving in with them. As they walked out, the realtor poked her head back in and asked, "How much do you want for this house?" Don smiled and said, "Make me an offer."

I was pretty surprised by all of this, and wasn't thrilled at the thought of moving … again. I asked Don, "What do you want for the house?" He told me an exact amount he was thinking, and said if we could get that amount, he would sell it.

A couple of days later, our lives got turned upside-down in a moment and the thought of selling our house went completely out of our minds. I was out running some errands and turned my cell phone off thinking no one needed me at that time of day. Later, as I was busily doing laundry, someone began pounding on my front door. It was my friend, Smyrna, who was on staff at our church and helped me with the women's ministry.

"Where have you been?" she blurted out. "We have been trying to reach you! Don is in the emergency room and is seriously ill. Come with me. I will drive you there." Needless to say, I rarely turn my cell phone off any more.

We raced to the hospital. Don had been having lunch with one of our church elders when he suddenly started coughing up quite a bit of bright red blood. The elder knew he needed to get Don help quickly. So he threw some money on the table for their lunch, grabbed Don, and headed for the nearest emergency room.

When I arrived, things were pretty serious. Don had been sick with the flu four months earlier, which left him with a bad cough; it was now February. Every so often, I would say, "You need to see a doctor if that cough doesn't go away." But then the next day it would seem better, so he never went.

His right lung was now hemorrhaging, and the blood was beginning to spill over from his right lung into his left lung. He was drowning. The medical staff irrigated his lungs, hoping to stop the bleeding. After a few hours they decided he was stable enough to send him home since the bleeding had stopped. We were instructed to go to Good Samaritan Hospital in the morning to find out the cause of the bleeding. As we were leaving, I apprehensively asked, "What if he starts coughing up blood again? What should I do?" They told us if that happened, we needed to get him to the hospital as fast as possible.

We went home and Don went to bed. We were both pretty concerned—actually, I was pretty scared. I fed him a light supper

THE TRUNK

of soup and then he began coughing again, and the bleeding started again. I flew into my jeans and raced for the hospital with Don in tow.

They took him in quickly and put him in a bed in the emergency room. The admitting doctor looked extremely concerned and sympathetic. The look on his face said, *This doesn't look good.*

I went out to call Michael and Brenda to ask them to come down to the hospital (they wouldn't allow me to use my cell phone inside the hospital). When I came back into the room, I was greeted by a scene of chaos. We had almost lost him! The man in the bed next to Don was dying, and all of the medical staff were trying to save him.

As this was happening, Don began to code. All of the color had drained from his face as he was slipping into unconsciousness. He actually felt his heartbeat stop, but was too weak to call for help. All of the medical staff was just behind the curtain next to him but had no idea what was happening to him. Just at the critical moment a nurse walked by and saw his ashen face. They immediately went to work to revive him and were able to save him. They kept him stable until morning when more tests could be run to find out the source of the bleeding.

In the morning, X-rays showed something that looked like a tumor. *Was it cancer?* They were not sure, but they wanted to operate as soon as they could set it up.

Our other two sons had moved to Southern California. I quickly called them, and Don's parents and siblings. His brother-in-law and sister had a plane. So they flew our boys and our parents up that morning. It didn't look good.

Amazingly, Don was at total peace. He knew he may not make it. He told the doctor if he didn't, not to worry—he had prepared for this his whole life and he would be with the Lord. The doctor, not a believer, said, "Hold that thought! I wish all my patients felt that way!"

During the surgery they had to remove the bottom section of his right lung. Bronchitis had eaten a hole in the main artery, and that was the cause of the profuse bleeding. We rejoiced that the cause was found, and that it was not cancer.

After surgery when he was in recovery and not fully conscious, his mother and sister, Marilyn, and our oldest son, Marcus, went in to see him. They had to return to Southern California, and I wanted them to see him before they left. I watched from the hallway because they would only allow three people in the room for short periods of time.

As I watched, Don's eyes were shut. He was still very out of it, but the other three in the room were in tears. As he lay there, he was saying something and they were listening intently. I found out later that he was quoting Scripture from Psalm 139.

If you remember, a couple of years earlier, Don had a stroke in his right eye and lost most of the vision in that eye. Once this happened, he felt compelled to memorize Scripture. He thought, *If something happens to my other eye, I want to have as much Scripture as possible already in my heart and mind.* So he began memorizing the book of Psalms. Then when he was in the hospital, barely coherent, he was quoting Psalm 139 from his heart.

All that you take in of God's Word will pour out of you in your hour of need. His Word is living and powerful (Hebrews 4:12). When you tuck God's Word away in your heart, it's always at your fingertips—whether you are witnessing, giving answers to people, or needing comfort yourself.

What a testimony this was to our family!

That next morning, I got up to fix breakfast and found Marcus and his friend, Mark Lugo, talking about the night before. Marcus was reading Psalm 139 to his friend, telling him about his dad quoting this passage.

Don had been memorizing the Psalms for months. They were buried in his mind and heart, and they surfaced in the hour he needed them. We all needed to hear them that day in the hospital.

The out-of-town family flew home and Don was resting in the hospital. I went home to get some sleep. I was exhausted, yet relieved that Don was going to get better though still very weak and not completely out of the woods yet. *Thank You, Jesus, You literally saved him!*

I crawled into bed, and the phone rang; it was the realtor. I had forgotten all about her. She told me that the young couple wanted to buy our house. To my utter amazement, their offer was the exact amount—to the dollar—Don had told me he would take for the house. Wow! Confirmed. I guess we were moving.

Don came home after a few days and rested at home. His roommate in the hospital had a cold! The doctor didn't think it was a good idea for him to be exposed to this right after surgery. All Don needed was another coughing spell with a cold after major lung surgery.

As Don was home recovering, the realtor came over and the deal was signed, right then and there, with no time wasted. I put a chair next to Don's bed for her and sat on the foot of the bed while Don laid there. I said, "Well, this is great! You and the realtor will make money, and Don is too sick to lift a box. So I guess I will be doing all the work." Don ended up hiring our sons to come and help us move. Poor guys!

I lay in bed and thought, *Where are we going to move to?* The following week, I went to church and watched a movie on creation and saw a beautiful picture of the earth from out in space—hung on nothing—perfect and beautiful. I said to my friend next to me, "Well, if God can do that, I guess He can find a house for us!"

He hangs the earth on nothing.
Job 26:7

He knows where we are to live and He will lead us.

20

He Knows Our Dwelling Place: Blain Court

*And He has made from one blood every nation of men to
dwell on all the face of the earth,
and has determined their preappointed times
and the boundaries of their dwellings.*
Acts 17:26

One day my friend, Tamara, called to tell me about a new housing development that was opening up in our area. The Lord had miraculously just sold our home, so we were now in need of a place to live. Does God really care where we live? I believe He does! My friend was going to go look at these new homes and encouraged us to look too. Best of all, they were practically across the street from our church.

THE TRUNK

I remember well the time that I asked two pastors' wives (Diane Coy and Carol Wild) to pray that we would find a home. They gave me the verse in the book of Acts that says, "And He has made from one blood every nation of man to dwell on all the face of the earth, and has determined their preappointed times and the boundaries of their dwellings" (Acts 17:26). I had never really thought that God would care about where we live, our dwelling place, but He does.

We went to look at the model homes as the houses hadn't even been built yet. San Jose had such a housing shortage at the time that certain days were set to put in a bid on the houses. The problem for us was that we were going to be in Florida on that day. We asked Michael and Brenda if they would go to the drawing for us; they said they would. When they arrived there were 150 people who were putting in their names and only ten lots (or houses) available. We really wanted Lot 21, which was in the back near the corner; it was a quieter section of the neighborhood. When the names were drawn, we were actually picked out for another lot, one we weren't crazy about. Our son and his wife sat there for a while wondering what to do. Two men who had also been picked were quietly talking nearby. Then they turned around to Michael and said, "Would you like Lot 21? We got it, but we heard it was on a flood plain, so we don't want it."

"Yes!" Michael said, "I'll take it." It was the exact lot we desired most. Michael went to the realtor and told her the situation, and that the man who had drawn Lot 21 said it was on a flood plain. She said, "No, it's not. I need to tell them." She went out to the parking area to find them, but they were nowhere to be found.

Needless to say, we were delighted that the Lord had given us Lot 21. With the small number of homes (only ten) compared with the large number of people vying for them, it was a wonder that we were even chosen at all—let alone, that we got the exact one we wanted. What are the chances of that?! God in His sovereignty had chosen our boundaries and our dwelling place. He sold our house and gave Don the desire of his heart—that is, to live near our church. This new neighborhood was practically across the street from our church.

But the story got even better. God provided extra little blessings that we could not have even imagined.

That year we celebrated Thanksgiving as we moved out of our little condo and into our Lot 21, which was now a lovely new home. All of our kids came to celebrate the holiday with us and make the house a home. We were truly thankful.

A couple of weeks before Christmas, Don was driving down the street and saw that they were tearing out all of the plants from the model homes. "What are you doing?" he asked. "Well," they said, "the boss said we had to take the landscaping out because these homes are to be sold just like the other homes with no backyard landscaping." That seemed very odd to Don, but he said, "If you are throwing them away, I'll pay you $150 to plant them in my yard." They checked with their boss and he agreed, and the workers made a little extra money in the process.

THE TRUNK

I had gone to the store and when I returned a couple of hours later I had a fully-planted beautiful yard with about nine trees and sixty bushes. *Wow! Thank You, Jesus—that was the best Christmas present ever!*

"He cares about the places of our dwellings." Such an amazing God we serve!

A couple of weeks later, Don once again drove by the model homes and the gardeners were putting in all new plants. "What are you doing?" Don asked.

"Well," they said, "the builder made a mistake and these model homes were supposed to be sold with the landscaping." Again I had to smile. The Lord is so good to us and cares about those little things that mean so much to us.

Does God care about the details of our lives? I believe He does and sometimes in the midst of the storms of life, He puts us in a peaceful and comforting place. No, we don't always get the Norman Rockwell life, but sometimes, by His loving grace, He gives us the Thomas Kinkade cottage. Isaiah 32:18 says, "My people will dwell in a peaceful habitation, in secure dwellings, and in quiet resting places."

Don had wanted to live near the church for a long time. When our house sold and he was in the hospital after surgery, I was alone at home one night when the Lord gave me James 5:16b: "The effective, fervent prayer of a righteous man avails much." God had truly answered Don's prayer.

21

The Pilgrim Years

*Blessed is the man whose strength is in You,
whose heart is set on pilgrimage.*
Psalm 84:5

When Jacob was asked how old he was, he told Pharaoh that the *years of his pilgrimage* were 130 years—I like that. When our citizenship is anchored in heaven, these days here on earth are simply our pilgrim years. This truth has become very real to me as I have entered another new phase in my life.

Our pilgrim years began without us even realizing it. We had been in San Jose for eleven years when Chuck Smith called Don and asked him to come back to Calvary Chapel of Costa Mesa to help him as he prepared to retire. Jon Courson (a friend and pastor who had served with us at Calvary in the early years) was coming back from Oregon to help as well. But as it turned out, Chuck was so refreshed by the growth and excitement at Calvary that he realized he wasn't ready to retire. And so the Lord moved us on after only one year. God brought us to a struggling church in Laguna Beach, California. They had lost their pastor and Chuck thought Don would be just the one to help. Over the years, Don had pastored four churches and helped start several others. Like San Jose, this church was going to need a lot of love and the Holy Spirit's healing touch to a hurting congregation.

Two short years later, we were in Boston at a pastors conference staying in a hotel when Don said, "I think the Lord wants us to leave the Laguna church and step out in faith to travel and speak." We were doing a lot of that anyway, and he felt we were to do this full-time.

The church in Laguna was healthy and thriving again. There was a feeling of stability, and the staff was happy. Several of our family members had been attending the church as well. *How would we tell them we were leaving them?* I felt sick at the thought. Don was actually writing out his resignation and emailing it to the board as I sat in the hotel room in Boston and prayed. *Give me something Lord—give me a Scripture!* In my devotions that morning I had read this verse: "Blessed is the man whose strength is in You, whose heart is set on pilgrimage" (Psalm 84:5). All I could see was my suitcase parked at the door of that hotel room. And for the last eight years it has pretty much been that way, and so I call these the pilgrim years of my life.

Don and I have collected enough frequent-flyer miles to go Diamond with Delta, and sometimes we get weary in the journey. I have found the key of this verse is where it says, "whose strength is in (the Lord)" (Psalm 84:5). God gives us His strength in those moments of our weakness. I have found Him to be faithful always.

When we first began our journey, we had one trip that was especially exhausting. We were flying on Southwest Airlines, and it was a full flight. I was riding in one of those seats that faces backwards and was getting a headache. Then, on the next flight, a child cried and screamed throughout the flight, and his mother couldn't quiet him. I felt ill. I turned to Don in between the child's screams and said, "I don't know if I can do this and travel like this."

He said, "Then don't come with me." I was hoping for sympathy, but that is not what I got from him. Maybe he was just as exhausted as me. As I sat there, I really thought about what he said and knew it was from the Lord. It reminded me of my dad telling me when I went to boarding school at age fourteen to not complain—no matter what was put in front of me.

The Lord was teaching me in the beginning of our pilgrim years that I must just trust Him and go, and not complain. Complaining makes you, and everyone else around you, miserable.

If I tell Jesus my needs, He will take care of me. I don't need to complain about them to others.

THE TRUNK

*My flesh and my heart fail; but God is the strength of
my heart and my portion forever.*
Psalm 73:26

On another such trip, we were flying a red-eye from California to Florida for the weekend and then back to Los Angeles (LAX), late at night. We had to catch an early morning flight to our next destination the following day. Our plane was held up on the tarmac at LAX and all I could think about was crawling into bed. I was running on empty, but there was no use in complaining to Don because he was just as tired. So I sat there staring blankly out the window and complained to God.

Please, Lord. I am exhausted. I just need a bed and some sleep. You promised me Your strength. I really need some of that right now.

When we finally got off the plane, we only had a few hours to sleep at a nearby hotel, and then we caught another flight to travel 2,400 more miles. The next day, when we were settled at our next stop, I received a text from a dear friend (and fellow pastor's wife) who knew nothing about my prayer or our current situation. Her message read, "Your God has commanded your strength" (Psalm 68:28). How amazing! A friend thousands of miles away, who I hadn't talked to in days, sent me the words I needed. I felt so loved by God as I was reminded of His strength being commanded toward me.

During this season we spent three weeks each month away from home. One week was spent working with Potter's Field Ministries in Montana, and eventually Guatemala, and on various missions' trips. The Lord also led us to help our dear friends, Joe and Cathy Focht, at Calvary Chapel of Philadelphia for two weeks of the month. God guided our steps and continued to confirm that our travel was His will for this time. Three times He gave me the verse about being willing to leave family and home for the sake of the gospel: twice in my devotions and once in a Sunday morning sermon. The message was a clear, "Go."

And everyone who has left houses or brothers or sisters or
father or mother or wife or children or lands,
for My name's sake, shall receive a hundredfold,
and inherit eternal life.
Matthew 19:29

So we continued to travel and as my dear friend, Gail Mays, said to me, "Just trust God and go." In Psalm 138:3 it says, "In the day when I cried out, You answered me, and made me bold with strength in my soul."

Prevailing in Prayer

Prayer will carry you through difficult times; it will be worth the agony and anguish in the end. Sometimes, casual, ordinary prayer isn't enough, and God calls us to prevailing prayer; this kind of prayer comes when you are in deep distress. *Webster's Dictionary* defines the word *travail* as: "To work, especially of a painful or laborious nature; physical, mental exertion or piece of work. Its synonyms are agony, anguish, hurt, distress, and pain.

We as Christians are called to carry our cross, to carry the burdens of others to Him, and it is agonizing sometimes. My mother and mother-in-law both got up every morning at 5:00 a.m. to pray—they were women of travailing prayer. They actually ended up meeting each other at a ladies' prayer meeting. I always think that much of God's work in and through Don and I and our children is only because of the prayers of our mothers—two prayer warriors. And whether or not you had a godly mother or father, you can be that for the next generation. "My house shall be called a house of prayer" (Isaiah 56:7). Don't sell prayer short.

Heavy Burdens

Our son and his wife were heading into a terrible divorce. I kept thinking that this can't be happening to our family. I prayed and begged God to fix things in their marriage, yet the divorce came.

I was home alone one afternoon when the doorbell rang. A man said he had a registered letter for us; it was divorce papers being served to our son. *Why me?* I thought. *Why not my son or husband? Why do I have to be the only one home to accept these papers?* I could hardly bear it. Perhaps God knew they couldn't take it either, and so that left me. I was so heartbroken and ashamed at the thought of one my children getting divorced. We are a minister's family. How could this be happening to us?

I stood there hoping the delivery guy didn't know who we were. As I was thinking this, he looked intently at me and said, "Isn't your husband, Don McClure, on the radio?" I stared in fear for a second because I didn't want anyone to know our family was going through a divorce. Slowly, I answered, "Our family is going through a very difficult time right now." Then he said, "I am a Christian, and I go to Calvary Chapel. My friends and I will pray for you." His words were words of comfort to a broken soul.

"Thank you," I said. "You don't know what that means to me right now." I knew just then God had sent him. Whatever we go through, especially the worst moments in our lives, He has not forgotten us nor left us alone, but He always sends His children to remind us of His presence.

I would wake up at three or four in the morning for months and couldn't go back to sleep. I wanted to fix these hurting hearts and turn them around before more people got hurt. The burden was almost unbearable at times. Like the movie, *Back to the Future,* faces were disappearing from my family photograph. The Lord actually gave me a vision of that, like a warning, before it all happened.

Not long after that, I was crying one day as I was cleaning the kitchen floor. I asked God, "What will become of my grandchildren? Divorce will cause irreparable damage. Will they grow up and not know You or be bitter toward You?" Just then, that still, quiet voice spoke to my heart, "Why are you crying?" God whispered. "Are the children healthy?"

"Yes," I answered.

"Are they handicapped? Are they ill?"

"No, Lord."

"Then why are you crying? Did they accept Me when they were very young?" I remembered Chase, the oldest, sitting in church at two years old with his parents listening to the worship songs.

"Yes, Lord."

"You don't know their end!"

Then I knew I could trust Him with the children. I did not know where their lives would go—they were so little—but I knew Who held them in His hand. As I continued cleaning my kitchen floor, I began to sing praises to Him.

*Come to Me, all you who labor
and are heavy laden, and I will give you rest.*
Matthew 11:28

Two years later, in July of 2006, we went to visit our grandchildren in Florida. They had moved three thousand miles away. We were able to be with them for three days. During our brief visit we took them to Disney World and out to eat. The second day we were together, the Lord gave me a verse in my morning devotions from Isaiah. It said, "It shall come to pass in that day that his burden will be taken away from your shoulder, and his yoke from your neck, and the yoke will be destroyed because of the anointing oil" (Isaiah 10:27). The oil of the Holy Spirit is like salve to our wounds, and I felt it wash over me.

At the end of our trip, I walked out the door of their house to our car and suddenly I realized I wasn't crying anymore. I remembered the verse from the day before and knew that God had lifted my burden. I told the Lord, "They are Yours, Lord. I put them in Your hands, each of them. Please take care of them for me." I remember telling Elle, the youngest, I never wanted to get to heaven and find any of them missing. I would never stop praying for them. I love them dearly.

Cancer

Six years later, during our time of traveling, I went in for my annual mammogram between trips. I almost canceled the appointment because we were so busy, but I had a strong impression to "just do it." Having that simple test saved my life. Soon after the mammogram, they called me back for another test. I remember the doctor saying, "You are probably fine. It is most likely nothing, but just to be sure I want you to go get a biopsy." I noticed the expression of the nurse standing behind him, and her face said it all: concern and fear for me. I have learned to watch the nurse's faces—they tell all.

They ran me through the system in record time to fit with our scheduled flights. One afternoon I was waiting for the doctor's call to hear the results of the biopsy and wanted Don to be with me when the call came. We were having company for dinner the next day, and I couldn't wait any longer to run out for groceries. I remember getting into my car and backing out of the garage when my phone rang. Thankfully, Don had come out front and was standing beside my car as I answered it; it was the doctor.

"Hello," he said. "We have your test results."

"You didn't find anything," I said anxiously, "right?"

THE TRUNK

"Actually, we did," he said.

"It was just pre-cancer, right?" I said.

"No, actually, you have cancer," he answered.

At that moment in time, everything seemed to stand still; it felt like I was in a dream—a nightmare actually—and that it couldn't be real.

"I am seeing my last patient at 4:00 p.m. today," the doctor said. "When can you get here?"

"My husband and I will be there at 4:30 p.m."

Don and I walked back into the house in complete shock and stunned silence. Life is tough, but God is good—and this was one of those moments. Then Don said, "I just wish this was me and not you." I love him so much. My dear husband was going through this with me. He had gone through many life-threatening, painful things, but it was so hard for him to not be able to fix this for me and keep me from suffering.

The day after I was told it was cancer, I called my mother-in-law to tell her the news. She had such a positive attitude, full of hope. She said that the Lord had already been impressing a verse on her heart, and now she knew it was for me. She said God would hold me by His strong right hand (see Isaiah 41:10).

Three weeks before my surgery, I woke up at 3:30 a.m. unable to sleep. So I opened the Bible to find my comfort there and listen for God to speak to me. Scripture after Scripture spoke directly to my heart. I remember being struck by Jesus telling His disciples to ask Him their petitions or needs. Jesus said, "Therefore I say to you, whatever things you ask when you pray, believe that you receive them, and you will have them" (see Mark 11:22-24). Then I read the verse that says, "You do not have because you do not ask" (James 4:2). So I prayed, *Lord, don't let it be cancer if this is Your will.*

But I have learned that sometimes He says, *No,* and that is His will for the situation. He allows certain trials for a reason—to comfort others.

> *Blessed be the God and Father*
> *of our Lord Jesus Christ,*
> *the Father of mercies and God of all comfort,*
> *who comforts us in all our tribulation,*
> *that we may be able to comfort those*
> *who are in any trouble, with the comfort with which we*
> *ourselves are comforted by God.*
> 2 Corinthians 1:3-4

God said *No.*

Three days before my surgery, I read Ecclesiastes 7:14 which says, "In the day of prosperity be joyful, but in the day of adversity consider: surely God has appointed the one as well as the other."

Paige—prosperity

Cancer—adversity

Paige was my oldest granddaughter, who would soon be a great blessing to me from the Lord.

Cancer, on the other hand, would bring me pain and suffering.

Surely, God appointed one as well as the other.

In everything give thanks;
for this is the will of God in Christ Jesus concerning you.
1 Thessalonians 5:18 (KJV)

Over the next few weeks I would undergo major surgery and still continue to travel. In my weakness, a wheelchair was needed to get through the airports in Montana and Philadelphia. I didn't want to be away from Don, so I would travel with him and rest wherever he was working. As I chose to be thankful in everything, I began to notice things I hadn't seen much before. For example, Delta Airlines had breast cancer awareness month in October, and our flight attendant wore a pink dress. I found out that she was also a Christian. *How lovely,* I thought, *even Delta Airlines cares.*

I will never forget when Joe Focht picked us up at the airport in Philadelphia; he had tears in his eyes as I came through the door in that wheelchair. He had seen so much cancer and suffering in his own church, and it has made him deeply compassionate.

Some weeks after surgery, I went to the doctor and quietly observed my surroundings. When I returned home, I wrote about it in my journal. Here are my reflections from that day:

> I sit in the waiting area of my oncologist doctor's office. Having just had blood drawn, I watch others. There is a man sitting across from me. The nurse

drawing his blood said, "Hi Dave. How are you today?"

"Not so good," replied the elderly gentleman.

"Sorry to hear it," said the nurse slowly, calmly and compassionately; it takes a special nurse to work in oncology. The man closed his eyes and sat quietly. *Does he feel ill,* I wonder. His reports are not good, I am sure.

I looked at women across from me in another waiting area. Some look pretty sick—scarves, thinning hair, pale skin. *This really is an awful place, Lord. My heart is so sad for those around me. Cancer is a terrible disease. There is no laughter here. What am I thankful for? I know that the opposite of complaining is to be thankful.*

My heart goes out to my niece and three friends who have just been diagnosed with breast cancer. But I am thankful that God is doing miracles for them; they will live longer.

Don is in Africa on a mission trip, but God sent my children to live in town so I am near to them. I am thankful; it has always been my dream to be near my kids. *Thank You, Lord.*

I am blessed.

I am blessed with Paige, my granddaughter.

I am blessed with Don, who loves me.

I am blessed with family and dear friends.

I am blessed.

THE TRUNK

You are with me;
You have been every day, every step of the way.
You surround me with mercy.
I am blessed.

I am living in a suffering, dying world. Lord, help me reach out with Your love to those who are suffering.

O God, You have taught me from my youth; and to this day I declare Your wondrous works. Now also when I am old and gray-headed, O God, do not forsake me, until I declare Your strength to this generation, Your power to everyone who is to come.
Psalm 71:17-18

I must comfort others.

Paige

There was, however, a great treasure in this storm—a sweet miracle and answer to prayer. On my dresser I kept pictures of my children and grandchildren. Under my oldest granddaughter's (Paige) picture I had put a little silver frame with the words "all things" in it, taken from a verse in Mark 14:36, "And He said, "Abba, Father, *all things* are possible for You." Jesus was praying in Gethsemane to the God of the impossible.

Five years had passed from our trip to Florida to the week the doctor told me I had cancer. I pulled on my sweats and went for a walk. "Lord," I prayed. "If You said that nothing was impossible for Your Father to do, then surely it is true! You knew Your Father from the beginning. So please, Lord, could You go get Paige and bring her back to You, and back to us?"

My mother-in-law had been praying for the past couple years that someone would invite our grandkids to church. All three of them had been affected by the divorce, but for some reason, Paige went through it the worst. Her life had become a shipwreck. No child should ever have to go through the things Paige went through. On top of her life falling apart, she became a strong atheist, no longer believing in God. After all, He hadn't shown up to help her, or so she thought. Meanwhile, on that day in August as I walked, I prayed for her specifically. The very next day while I was on my walk my cell phone rang; it was Paige! I hadn't heard from her in months.

"Mimi," she said. "I have something to tell you. A friend took me to church. I sat in the back, and in my heart I was making fun of all those crazy Christians. Two weeks later, I was in the front row with tears running down my face and my hands lifted up to heaven. Mimi, I came back to God! I think I want to go around the world and tell people about Him."

Don, her papa, called her back and said, "Paige, Mimi and I work with a Christian organization called Potter's Field Ministries. We are going up to their ranch in Montana this Sunday. If you would be interested in going there, we will get you a plane ticket to meet us there."

THE TRUNK

Paige fasted and prayed for three days before responding to us. She felt God had told her to go. And as she puts it, at seventeen years old she left everything—college, her mother, her sister, her boyfriend, her job, her cat, and all her friends—and got on a plane to a place she had never been, to meet people she didn't know, to go to Bible school. But she did it! I was more than amazed at what God can do—the God who can do the impossible.

Not long after Paige arrived at Potter's Field Ranch, they had a midnight river trip—August summer nights in Montana were warm and wonderful. Paige and another student wanted to be baptized, so Mike Rozell baptized my granddaughter that night. I received a picture later from one of our friends, and it captured the moment beautifully. Paige came up out of the water with tears in her eyes and her hands raised to heaven. The moonlight was shining behind her; it was a priceless sight and an amazing testimony of God's redeeming grace. Paige asked Mike if he had baptized people before. He said, "Oh, yes ... but never like this one."

Eight months later she sat next to me on the front row at the women's seminar at Calvary Chapel of Philadelphia. During the closing worship song, she slid on to the floor on her knees, hands raised and tears running down her cheeks. I poked my friend, Cathy Focht, who was on the other side of me, to see Paige. For the last few years, Cathy and I sat in that seminar, in the same spot, and prayed for Paige. My friends, Sandy and June, who had prayed for her as well, were sitting behind us that night. What a joy it was to witness an amazing and overwhelming answer to our prayers right there in front of us. Never give up praying for your children and your loved ones. As long as there is breath, there is hope. May Paige's story encourage you to keep on praying!

Paige stayed at Potter's Field for almost two years, and then went to Calvary Chapel Bible College in Murrieta, California. Today she is about to get married to Jordan Grace, the man of her dreams. He is a godly man whose family is in ministry in Australia and the United States. His grandparents were missionaries to Papua New Guinea. God has given Paige a new name, Paige *Grace,* for certainly God's grace has been written over the pages of her new life. Oh, how that blesses my heart!

Paige called to tell me that she had come back to the Lord the same week I found out I had cancer. I remember one early morning after my surgery when it was still dark outside; I was lying in bed wondering about what would become of me. *How bad is this going to get?* I wondered. The doctor told me the day before that the cancer had gotten invasive. If I hadn't had that mammogram when I did, I wouldn't be here. As I lay in bed in the early morning hours, I heard God speak to me so clearly, not an audible voice, but very clear in my head.

He said, "Enjoy the journey."

Such peace flooded me I can't even explain it. I knew without a doubt that I was in His hands. If God could bring Paige back from three thousand miles away—and thousands of miles away from Him—He could take care of every cell in my body. His peace changed my perspective on all I was going through. I began to look for the miracles and blessings in this journey.

One afternoon I was all alone in my backyard and just started to cry. I think it was just pent-up emotion that let loose when I was by myself. At that very moment, a text came from my friend, Sandy MacIntosh, saying she was praying for me. I told her the text came at the very moment I needed it most. She said, "Consider it a kiss from Jesus." I love that! He has sent me many kisses along the way. He wanted me to notice—to look for Him—and enjoy the journey.

Another sweet kiss from Jesus during this difficult trial was my daughter-in-law, Erin. The Lord had allowed her and Don II to stay with us at this time. She is a skilled registered nurse who had been working in the oncology department at the hospital where I had my surgery. Her care for me was just what the Lord knew I needed—and so much more. What are the chances of having an oncology nurse staying with me at this time?

God was so sweetly faithful to me. He was walking through it with me and many times it felt like He was holding my hand. In His mercy, I have been cancer-free for three-and-a-half years now. I praise Him for the lessons learned during my health issues. He showed me that in the hurricanes of life, He can tuck us into the eye of the storm and give us peace and quiet no matter what is circling around us.

You will keep him in perfect peace, whose mind is stayed on You, because he trusts in You.
Isaiah 26:3

22

Final Reflections

*The God who has fed me
all my life long to this day.*
Genesis 48:15b

Don and I went to visit my dear mother-in-law in the Alzheimer's home recently. Dad passed away last year and Mom longs to go be with him. She is now ninety-two years old, and the dementia has gotten worse. But her moments of lucidity are wonderful. Jesus holds her spirit despite her frail mind, and once in a while, her thoughts are crystal clear. She never complains about anything, but is always grateful for all God has done for her and her family. Each time we visit her we walk away feeling blessed. On this day, as clear as could be, she said, "I have had a wonderful life. Don't cry when I am gone; for I will have graduated, and I am going to see my husband and the Lord. I will see you soon after … (she paused), but not too soon."

THE TRUNK

Meditate on the Miracles

In Genesis 48:15, Jacob was 147 years old and had come to the end of his life. Jacob had spent most of his life struggling with everyone around him; Jacob means *cheat*. So God broke him—He wrestled with him and gave him a limp as a realistic visual of complete dependency on God. He could not go on in his own strength and self-preservation any more. Through this need for dependency on God, He changed Jacob's name from cheating and plotting to the name Israel, which means governed by God. How like us Jacob was! When we come to the end of ourselves, we come to the beginning of God. God will take care of us. We don't need to scheme and plot and cheat to survive. We can simply trust Him to watch over us. Jacob knew this in the later years of his life. When he was giving his blessing to Joseph's two boys before he died, he referred to God as, "The God who has fed me all my life long" (Genesis 48:15b).

As I look back and sift through the memories that are in the trunk of my life, I too see that God has taught me, corrected me, broken me, kept me, loved me and mine, and fed me all the days of my life—physically and spiritually—and redeemed me from the enemy.

I shall forever be grateful.

> *But as for me, I would seek God,*
> *and to God I would commit my cause—*
> *who does great things, and unsearchable,*
> *marvelous things without number.*
> Job 5:8-9

FINAL REFLECTIONS

I wrote to my granddaughter, Paige, and told her to write down all of her miracles so that she can be encouraged on bad days. When she is old she can tell her children. We often miss the miracles because we either explain them away or we simply don't look for them. Look for the miraculous and remember to thank God. Perhaps you say, "I don't have any blessings. Life has been unfair and hard. God has done nothing for me."

If you cannot find anything to thank God for, you can thank Him for this: He died for you because He loves you, and that is your miracle!

> *I will remember the works of the LORD;*
> *surely I will remember Your wonders of old.*
> *I will also meditate on all Your work,*
> *and talk of Your deeds.*
> *Your way, O God, is in the sanctuary;*
> *who is so great a God as our God?*
> *You are the God who does wonders;*
> *You have declared Your strength among the peoples.*
> Psalm 77:11-14

My dad was right when he told me not to complain in this life. So I have picked up this treasure out of the trunk of my life—this important lesson—and I have been reminded of it many times. Instead of focusing on what is hard or challenging and complaining about these things, I have made a new one-liner for my life: I choose to

MEDITATE ON THE MIRACLES!

... and that brings great joy.

THE TRUNK

The goodness of God is our hope—the anchor of our soul—not necessarily the end of the matter. Look for the goodness of God in the press of life; it will be a great treasure in *your* journey.

Drawn by Paige Grace